BEYOND THE FACE

'*Beyond the Face* presents a theoretical and practical framework that explores the rich world of portraits and helps the reader look beyond the image into the very soul of another person. The book takes its position from the Judeo-Christian tradition and argues that a portrait has the potential to explore identity, build connection with others, break down prejudice and facilitate wholeness. To do this the author has developed a new and innovative three-step approach based on the practices of mindfulness, meditation and contemplation.

Beautifully illustrated and with fascinating background information, the author brings the portraits to life, helping the reader to see beyond an image into the life of the person; you feel you know them. This point of connection can challenge prejudice and build an appreciation of different ways of being human. This is so important in our fragile world with increasingly fragmented and isolated communities. Portrait artists offer us a door into the world of the other person, helping us look beyond the face.

Having worked through the practical examples in this book I can strongly recommend it. I found the approach to be transformational in my own spiritual journey, it provides a simple framework which can be applied across many contexts to build connections with unfamiliar people and a deeper appreciation of what it means to be fully human.'

Dr Anne Moseley,
Faculty member, Oxford Centre for Mission Studies

BEYOND THE FACE

Looking for the Soul in a Portrait

STEPHEN GIRLING

DARTON·LONGMAN+TODD

First published in 2024 by
Darton, Longman and Todd Ltd
Unit 1, The Exchange
6 Scarbrook Road
Croydon CR0 1UH

ISBN: 978-1-915412-69-0

A catalogue record for this book is available from the British Library.

Front Cover Illustration: Image of the author generated by the DaVinci AI image generator in the cubist style of Pablo Picasso.

Quotations from the Bible are taken from the New Revised Standard Version (Anglican).

Printed and bound in Great Britain by Short Run Press, Exeter

IN MEMORY

In loving memory of my dear mother and father

Diane Girling
18th December 1938 – 17th November 2023

Jimmy Girling
4th January 1932 – 17th February 2024

They showed me the face of God in Jesus who always looked *beyond the face* of the other person in kindness and respect.

'Sight. Not a slight thing to teach, this: perhaps, on the whole, the most important thing to be taught in the whole range of teaching. To be taught to read – what is the use of that, if you know not whether what you read is true or false? To be taught to think – nay, what is the use of being able to think, if you have nothing to think of? But to be taught to see is to gain word and thought at once, and both true.'

John Ruskin,
Inaugural speech at the
Cambridge School of Art (1858).

CONTENTS

LIST OF ILLUSTRATIONS

LIST OF ILLUSTRATIONS

All images used by permission of the copyright holders.

PREFACE

I have had a long-standing interest in religious Icons in the Christian church, and how they are used in worship and prayer. The germ of the idea for this book, which builds on the work of religious Icons, arose in a dissertation for a Masters in Theology, Imagination and Culture. The subject was portraits by Vincent van Gogh, painted in the South of France, and his aspiration to portray 'something of the eternal' using complementary colours. I explored the way in which the Christian faith of Van Gogh's early years and his evolving spirituality shaped these portraits, and how they could be used today as 'Icon-like' images. From these beginnings the way lay open to deeper engagement with the inner life of the subject of any portrait.

Such engagement requires patient attention. In 2021 I was forced into a slower rhythm of life by the COVID-19 pandemic and with a growing interest in mindfulness and meditation I had the opportunity to develop these early ideas. The three-step method outlined in the introduction and developed in Chapter 5 was trialled and refined to provide a tool with which anyone can choose to go *beyond the face* in a portrait to see 'something of the eternal' in the other person. My growing interest in the contemplative prayer of monastic spirituality (in the Western Christian tradition) provided a further impetus to look beyond the physical features of a face to the inner life beyond.

I write as a practising Christian and a priest in the Church of England. I do not assume readers will practise a religious faith of their own, but I write knowing that many people in modern Britain pray, and many would describe themselves as spiritual but not religious. I hope everyone will discover something applicable to themselves. While I quote words from the Holy Bible spoken by Jesus Christ and others (these being familiar sources for my own Christian faith and work), I acknowledge that texts of other religious traditions would have their own contribution to make.

Virtually all artistic references are from within the Western European tradition, this being my area of interest and experience, both professionally and personally.

I would like to thank all those who participated in the trial of the three-step method and all who attended workshops during the evolution of the book. Thanks are also due to those who acted as critical friends during the final stages of writing.

I am grateful to the National Portrait Gallery in London for making their images accessible online and to the Van Gogh Museum in Amsterdam for giving easy online access to Van Gogh's letters which were invaluable in the early stages of research.

I am also grateful to members of the StillWaters new monastic community in Bath UK, with whom I have journeyed into a deeper understanding of the relationship between the creative arts and contemplative prayer, often curating spaces in which meeting strangers brought insight and revelation.

Finally, I would like to thank my wife Diane for her extraordinary patience, for encouraging me to keep writing while working full-time as a priest at Bath Abbey.

INTRODUCTION

A LANDSCAPE OF CHANGING FACES

As the world gets 'smaller', strangers cross our paths in increasing numbers and their faces and behaviours reflect a diversity that previous generations rarely encountered. Population growth, human migration, and the widespread movement of people from rural to urban areas, are all sculpting a new social landscape. The way we communicate with others has also changed beyond recognition. In the digital worlds of broadcast media, social media and virtual working we are brought face to face with a staggering diversity of people of different looks, ethnicities, sexualities, genders, cultures, and religions. At the same time in this evolving landscape, equality and accessibility concerns (which often involve legislation), have been challenging us to think harder about how we relate to the strangers we face in daily life, rightly holding us to account for our words and our actions.

Questions of personal identity, of who we are in an ever more crowded and diverse world, press upon us and in our anxious state many of us, are inclined to retreat from strangers and surround ourselves with the safe and familiar faces of our 'tribe' – those like us who we like, and who like us. However, the Christian worldview, which has shaped Western civilisation, reminds us that each individual person is unique and precious, and we are invited to flourish in communities of God-given diversity. This innate instinct inclining us towards others unlike us, who are somehow intrinsically vital to our wellbeing, conflicts with the unseen and often insidious cultural forces that drive us away from them.

The forces that repel us from strangers are often tangibly felt (and gain traction), in the way we tell our history, promote celebrity, and consume information. The tragic death of George Floyd in the United States of America, at the hands of a white police officer, brought into sharp relief serious misgivings about how we in the United Kingdom memorialise historical figures connected with exploitation and racial injustice. These include former slave-trader Edward Colston (1636-1721) whose statue was toppled and unceremoniously dumped into Bristol harbour in June 2020. Then in the much-vaunted hyper-real culture of Hollywood celebrity the #MeToo movement gained significant momentum as it exposed harassment and sexual abuse in the industry. These were the tragic consequence of years of subtly legitimised demeaning and denigrating behaviour. While both the Black Lives Matter and #MeToo movements have been greatly assisted by social media, it has become increasingly plain to see the toxic consequences of its lack of regulation. Unseen and untold damage is being caused by strangers (and strangers disguised as friends), who manipulate and abuse through these online platforms. The reinforcement of disdain, suspicion, and enmity towards those not of our 'tribe' is one of the pernicious side-effects of the algorithms that drive much of their content, feeding us what our lustful eyes want to see, and our itching ears want to hear.

However much the social climate in the United Kingdom is promising change for the better in response to these cultural forces, there remain significant inequalities and the 'othering' of those unlike us. Apart from gender and racial issues there remain ever more pressing questions about who we welcome to our shores and uncertainty about how we respect cultural and religious differences within our understanding of what it means to be British. All these are very live and important challenges, they directly impinge on our sense of who we are and who others are *beyond the face,* and how we can flourish together in our glorious diversity. Their pressing urgency has given added momentum to this book.

By looking harder at ourselves and others we will discover who we truly are, perhaps for the first time, and we will have the wherewithal to continue this adventure of discovery in this ever-evolving landscape. In Chapter 1 we will consider how images of the face have historically both reflected and shaped our self-understanding and our understanding of others and in Chapter 2 we will explore what it means to be human, with a body and soul, and how our well-being is influenced by our relations with others. These others will include those who are like us, whose images we collect, and those who are unlike us, to whom we previously might not even have given a second glance. We will discover how it is often strangers who help us see our flaws and help us discover deeper aspects of human flourishing than we could ever have discovered among the familiar faces of our 'tribe'.

LOOKING TO GO BEYOND THE FACE

A portrait artist has the opportunity to capture the face of their subject and to go further – to the person *beyond the face*, to communicate something much greater than their physical features. One artist with such an aspiration has been instrumental to the themes of this book. Vincent van Gogh specifically articulated his desire to go beyond the physical features of the face:

> *in a painting I'd like to say something consoling, like a piece of music. I'd like to paint men or women with that je ne sais quoi of the eternal, of which the halo used to be the symbol, and which we try to achieve through the radiance itself, through the vibrancy of our colorations … Ah, the portrait – the portrait with the model's thoughts, his soul – it so much seems to me that it must come.* (1) 3 Sept 1888

What had shaped Van Gogh's aspiration? As a young man he had embarked on a career as a Christian Evangelist, living after the example of Jesus among labourers and their families in Southern Belgium. In a letter to his brother he reflected on the street-sweepers, dustmen and coal miners among whom he lived and worked:

> *It always strikes me, and it is very peculiar, that when we see the image of unutterable and indescribable desolation – of loneliness, poverty and misery, the end*

or extreme of all things — the thought of God comes into our minds. At least it does with me. (2) 15 November 1878

Because of his Christian faith, Van Gogh understood that the people he served were as much made in the image of God as he was and that their abject poverty was an offence against God. He sought to right this wrong by personally meeting their needs for food, shelter and clothing, helping them as Jesus would have done.

However, a few years later, disenchanted by religion and the failure of his vocation as an Evangelist, Van Gogh moved to the South of France as an artist. His vocation to serve the poor was sublimated into the making of portraits of ordinary people from daily life — at least those who were willing to pose for him. These were friends and strangers he met in the cafes and bars he frequented and other acquaintances he made. Van Gogh may have turned his back on religion but he remained attuned to the spiritual dimension in nature and in other people. He had an extraordinary ability to see the person *beyond the face*, to paint consoling portraits of men and women by capturing something of their inner life. Chapter 3 of this book explains how Van Gogh did this by using complementary colours and explores the distinctive devices used by other portrait artists. These methods make portraits from any era full of possibility if we are willing to be intentional in our desire to go *beyond the face* to the inner world of another person.

Van Gogh was painting at a time when Europe was searching for its soul in the period of so-called enlightenment. After his death, Van Gogh's work finally received public acclaim and since then successive world wars, globalisation and climate change have given exceptional urgency to that same nagging question he had faced up to: what it means to be human in relation to those who are unlike us and in relation to the natural world.

In the shifting sands of public anxiety, social awareness and contested worldviews, the National Portrait Gallery in London has addressed this same question by encouraging portrait artists to experiment with the genre, to break away from the strictures of previous generations, just as Van Gogh had done. Since its inception the gallery had commissioned portraits which celebrated those who had made a significant contribution to the nation's history, to showcase those widely acclaimed as the 'great and the good'. In recent years there has been a deliberate shift towards accepting and commissioning portraits which reflect and contribute to narratives of social change. Visitors can see faces which have become familiar on our television screens and smartphones, those who contribute to the fabric of our lives and to our sense of belonging and well-being. These include sports personalities, musicians, people in the front line of education and healthcare and many other ordinary people who have in some way served the common good. Some of these and the devices used by artists to bridge the frontier between the seen and the unseen, are explored in Chapter 3 and are offered for practice and experiment in Chapter 6.

FROM RELIGION TO SPIRITUALITY

The twentieth-century decline of the all-prevailing hegemonic Christian worldview was mirrored in a shift from collective religion to individual spirituality and a democratisation of faith and learning. As church attendance in the United Kingdom has declined almost inexorably from the 1960s, interest in spirituality has grown, prompting Professor Grace Davie to suggest that people:

> believe without belonging, they are spiritual but not religious. (3)

INTRODUCTION

In the social landscape, two core spiritual values remain which are important in the main religious traditions of the United Kingdom. First, that humans are spiritual beings and secondly that we flourish best in community, we are a relational species. It is these two values that shape the substance of this book: we are all constituted by body and soul and we remain a stranger to others and to our truer selves unless we make the effort to pay attention to who we all are *beyond the face.*

As our population grows and becomes more and more diverse, there is an urgent need for these values to permeate how we see ourselves, and our relations with others. In our national life, the Archbishop of Canterbury, the Most Reverend Justin Welby, has been a passionate advocate for celebrating differences between people and for working to break down harmful barriers. He is committed to helping people with different beliefs and values to disagree well and to accept the fact that we don't need to be trying to convert the other person to our point of view. Instead, he advocates allowing a greater truth (above and beyond both of us) to reconcile, helping each of us value the differences between us, a philosophy based upon the example of Jesus. Jesus went out of his way to cross cultural and religious divides, to break down barriers created by wealth, gender, power, religion, age and race in order to go *beyond the face* of those for whom he felt compassion. When those who met Jesus recognised their need for a change of heart and mind to address barriers of difference, it was because they had been exposed to a greater truth embodied in his life and teaching: the truth that God is love and his love is indiscriminate. This unaffected and unconditional love of Jesus proved to be a powerful influence upon the lives of those he met. This is a love which can easily become obscured when religion is corrupted by power and suspicion, as church history has demonstrated. However, because it is a love at the very core of life itself, it remains alive and accessible in the spirituality of religion.

Portrait artists have furnished us with the images with which to transcend or break down barriers of difference and in the spirituality of religion we have the means to do so, the tools to go *beyond the face*. Mindfulness, meditation, and contemplation are explored in Chapter 4; they help us properly to see and relate to these faces, images of embodied spiritual beings like us. As we engage intentionally and meaningfully with portraits, we will in the process discover more of who we truly are as we give our attention to both our inner journey as embodied spiritual beings and our outer journey in lived experience with others.

INTRODUCTION

We have the images, and we have the tools, how are we going to use them? The answer (explored in Chapter 5) has been derived from Van Gogh's aspiration to paint *men or women with that je ne sais quoi of the eternal, of which the halo used to be the symbol.* For centuries religious artists have used the halo to identify Saints of the church. With their iconography they aim to lead religious believers *beyond the face* of the Saint, to where difference and discrimination are faded by the love of the Jesus they honour. These Saints are men and women officially recognised by the church as having honoured Jesus (or God) with their lives, and by whom or in whose name supernatural events have been witnessed (mostly miracles of healing). However, the church also considers anyone who aspires to live according to the example of Jesus to be a saint. We may not gain notoriety or have miracles attributed to us; however, we find our identity and purpose in honouring the life and teachings of Jesus. In his portraits from Southern France, Van Gogh painted faces of such saints, ordinary men and women steeped in the culture and practices of Roman Catholicism and with whom he had an intimate connection as a fellow spiritual human being.

INTRODUCING THE THREE-STEP METHOD

One artistic and religious discipline which makes systematic use of the halo is that of Icon writing (most commonly found within the Eastern Orthodox branch of the Christian church). Icons are 'written' in the sense that they follow an agreed grammar, and they are used by religious believers according to certain rituals of the church which help bridge the chasm between the temporal and eternal, the observer and the observed. It is these rituals that form the basis for the method outlined in Chapter 5 for going *beyond the face* of a portrait.

The method involves three steps:

Step 1: Looking – to Notice
Based upon mindfulness this step involves resisting all attempts to analyse the portrait, simply noticing what we see, in both broad and detailed observations.

Step 2: Looking – to Respond
Based upon meditation this step involves finding out what we can about the person in the portrait (and the artist), and with this knowledge then taking a fresh look to notice how we are responding. Once again, it's

important to resist all attempts at analysis of either the portrait or ourselves.

Step 3: Looking – to Reflect

Based upon meditation and contemplation this step involves looking again at the portrait as we harness our powers of thought, imagination, instinct, and intuition; analysing and reflecting upon the responses in Step 2. The aim is to identify what these responses tell us about ourselves and the person in the portrait, to celebrate differences and overcome barriers.

In its development the three-step method was trialled in two stages, using the portraits in Chapter 6. In the first stage, twenty participants individually completed the process with one of a choice of portraits and fed back detailed responses through a questionnaire. In the second, sixty participants participated in one of three workshops at which they were introduced to the method before using it on a single portrait, in a shared learning process.

Both stages revealed how hard people found Step 1. The vast majority had been schooled in analytical methods of art appreciation which focus on questions like: *What does it mean?* and *Why did they choose to do that?* Participants found it difficult to lay aside such questions in order simply to notice, without analysis. It required effort and self-discipline.

Some participants in the trials were unsure about whether they needed to engage with portraits in the way being proposed. They didn't necessarily have a desire to live differently or in any better way in respect to strangers with whom they differed. Some were diffident about a Christian perspective that made presumptions about the spiritual dimension of life. Curiosity and a willingness to have a go, with 'nothing to lose', are perhaps the best antidotes to these perfectly reasonable concerns.

The overtly cerebral nature of participants' engagement with the practice portraits led to a refinement of the method, with the introduction of contemplation into Step 3. Contemplation is the necessary approach for the worshipper looking at a religious Icon and is challenging for a Western mindset conditioned to success and worthwhile results. Though an unnatural discipline for many, contemplation values the practice of engagement more than the result – it helps us see beyond 'first sight', to become more present to others unlike us or who we don't like. Trial participants were almost unanimous in their opinion that though it takes practice, the three-step method is a useful tool with which to go *beyond the face* of a portrait.

The author's desire is that once the basic tools of

the method have been mastered with portraits, they will then have application in the wider world outside of the portrait – in our relations with those whose paths we cross in everyday life. Given the social landscape in the United Kingdom described earlier, we will have been helped both to know ourselves better and we will have cultivated kinder and more generous relations with others. With the rich and complex diversity of people in the United Kingdom this book aims to help us become intentional and more confident in transcending barriers, eradicating prejudice and getting to know others better.

BEYOND THE FACE

CHAPTER 1

HOW OTHERS SEE US

A BRIEF HISTORY OF PORTRAITS

Making a representation of the face has been an abiding fixation since the advent of image making in prehistory. In the Graeco-Roman era, busts and statues of emperors and philosophers served to remind the public of those who held ultimate authority. In early Christianity, the faces of Christ, his mother Mary and the Saints led people into worship and companionship within what is called the 'great communion of saints', those (dead and alive) who name themselves as followers of Jesus Christ. In the Renaissance, as European wealth increased so did the penchant for the newly rich to commission portraits of themselves as a way of flaunting their status. This burgeoning trade, together with the new medium of oil paint with its greater versatility, afforded the portrait artist of the fifteenth century a prominent position in the service of the royal court, the church and wealthy families. Many of these artists have become household names all over Europe; they include Leonardo da Vinci, Tiziano Vecellio (also known as Titian) and Giovanni Bellini – their skill and craft have literally fleshed out and given personality to those who helped shape the twists and turns of European history. However extraordinary their talent, they were working in an art-world largely dominated by the traditional rigid realism of the genre.

The widespread availability of the portrait grew in the fifteenth and sixteenth centuries with the arrival of the printing press and rapidly expanded with the advent of photography in the nineteenth century. In reaction to the realism of historic tradition, the royal academies and photography, the avant-garde artists of the nineteenth and early twentieth centuries offered us portraits that began to probe the nature of the person beyond the face; a person with a physical nature, a soul and a lived history. Van Gogh encapsulated this new and more honest approach to the person behind the face, painting many portraits of friends and acquaintances, including the local postmaster in Arles, Joseph Roulin **(Figure 1)**.

We see a similar representation of the true person in portraits by, for example, Edgar Degas, Paul Gaugin and

Edouard Manet. Their subjects were almost invariably not from the higher social classes but ordinary people; those who worked the land, who frequented cafes and bars and who plied their city trades. If a picture paints a thousand words, these nineteenth-century artists paved the way for portraits to explore realms beyond the immediate two-dimensional surface, in a manner already well established in myth, poetry, and metaphor.

As the insights of psychoanalysis gained traction in the early-twentieth century, amidst the tragic realities of two world wars, a period of intense soul-searching began over the woeful state of the human condition. The modern art movement played its part, a few examples will have to suffice:

- Pablo Picasso's (1881-1973) cubist portraits toyed with narrative and perspective to explore the constraints and possibilities of seeing beyond that which immediately presents itself.

- Frida Kahlo's (1907-1954) surrealist portraits probed the relations between physiology, lived history and personhood.

- To explore the painful and darker aspects of the human condition, Francis Bacon (1909-1992) introduced extremes of distortion to his portraits, giving a visceral energy to inner psychological anguish **(Figure 2)**.

- Jenny Saville's (b.1970) portraits, often larger than life, display large areas of flesh to accentuate embodied personality and to challenge prevailing stereotypes of beauty.

- With the rapid commercialisation of art in the 1960s, Andy Warhol (1928-1987) repeated and manipulated portraits within a single image to expose the vanity of a widespread exploitation of the human face.

We have been hard-pressed by the question of what it means to be human in the modern world and in response artists have left us with a rich legacy of portraits with which to go *beyond the face*.

PORTRAITS PRESENT AND FUTURE

Twentieth-century artists were engaging with the disquieted self-reflective mood of Western men and women grappling with the social forces of post-war reconstruction, post-industrialism, technological advances, and secularisation. Their work gradually moved further and further into public and private spheres through the rapid commercialisation of art and as people found themselves with more disposable income and time for learning, leisure and self-help. By the end of the century the average Westerner was richer, more healthy, better groomed, and much better educated than their forebears. However, as we looked at our pampered faces in the mirror, we found ourselves progressively gripped by the stark realities of self-doubt, insecurity, loneliness, and fear.

In this anxious world and with the new millennium upon us, nothing could have prepared us for the proliferation of images of the human face as digital media became democratised by growing availability, affordability, and advances in technology. If photography made the portrait much more widely accessible, the smartphone made it pervasive. Despite all the benefits of technology one unfortunate consequence has been the impact of software advances for digital manipulation which make possible the creation and curation of portraits like those of the pre-modern era, which mask the true person *beyond the face*. By the early-twenty-first century most Westerners, even before their early teens, had easy access to the tools with which to become their own portrait artist.

Self-portraiture has been a challenging genre of abiding interest, however the digital self-portrait, the 'selfie' (usually taken with a smartphone), exploded in popularity with the arrival of the front-facing camera in 2010. By 2013 the technology giant Apple claimed that more photos were being taken by their iPhone than by any other camera in the world. Since the advent of the selfie, software for airbrushing and name tagging faces, recording date and location and for the application of filters and image overlays, has made the portrait and self-portrait a constant feature of everyday life in the Western world. What is *beyond the face* in these portraits is usually the more superficial and everyday scenes of food, fashion, leisure, family, and friendship, rather than those of the subject's true psychological and spiritual state. However, what is superficial to one is affecting to another; we should not rule out the possibility that these selfies may also be helpful for going *beyond the face*. At the same time, we should not be blind to the shadow side of the selfie-culture which reveals itself in the urge to make and curate selfies that will be 'liked' and that fit with peer-approved body shape, size, complexion, and fashion. We are finding it increasingly straightforward and tempting to create and circulate images of the non-anxious, happy and beautiful selves we want others to see.

Over the same period in which the smartphone portrait became ubiquitous in the Western world, the need for safeguarding in public spaces, the threat of identity theft and the urgency of unmasking terrorists hiding in public view have made the image of the face virtually indispensable for public and private security. At the same time the war between secularism and religious freedom has raged on and has forced European governments to wrestle with the rights of their citizens to obscure their faces behind religious headwear. Personal liberty and freedom of expression have politicised the human face.

Similar issues have arisen around the use of facial recognition hardware and software for digital payment, smartphone security, location access and border control. In a very short space of time, images of our faces have become a highly valuable (and tradable) asset. Portraits and self-portraits are no longer the preserve of the domestic setting and the gallery; more than ever they are inextricably attached to the question of identity. Who we are is no longer simply a matter of idle curiosity, it is now also a matter of personal liberty and for some, life or death.

As if such issues weren't complex enough, in recent years have been added the impacts of health and safety concerns. In 2020 we saw the first formal and informal portraits in the United Kingdom of people wearing face coverings as protection against the COVID-19 virus. Almost overnight, recognising faces in public was no longer instant and the wearing of a face-covering was considered to be an act of benevolent regard for those vulnerable to infection.

As the threat of COVID-19 receded and face-coverings became optional rather than mandatory, as if from nowhere the software algorithm triggered a new threat to our ability to see the true person *beyond the face*. Digital tools for image manipulation which harness artificial intelligence to manipulate images of the human face are making it even more difficult to see who we and others are. The image on the front cover of this book was produced by an easily-accessible digital application which takes user-inputted keywords to create and refine images of the human face, either from a 'blank canvas' or from an existing image. In this instance the application was given a 'blank canvas' and over the course of ten minutes and three iterations was tasked to create a portrait using the following keywords: *portrait / Revd Stephen Girling / Vicar at Bath Abbey / inside the church / in the cubist style of Pablo Picasso.* It may not come even close to that which Picasso would have painted from a face-to-face sitting nevertheless it *is* a portrait fashioned by the creative interaction of the designers of the software and the author. While mildly amusing it makes the point. However, a more sinister reality is now at hand: the ability of algorithms to create 'deep fakes' – images of the human face intended to deceive. These deep fakes tell us little or nothing about the subject that is true to who they are, they mask an (often malicious) intent of their creator.

In our advanced and well curated worlds, we have the best images of others to keep us amused and of ourselves to keep us in favour with our peers. We can access these images whenever and wherever we want, and we might even believe we can control who we see and how others see us. Facial-recognition technology ensures our security and face-coverings protect our health; our life is in order, what more could we want? A whole lot more as it turns out. There has been a growing sense that there is more to being human than living in a technologically advanced and well-curated world. We are rediscovering contentment in mature relations to our self, to others (especially those unlike us), and for those who are spiritually inclined, to God. Perhaps the more important question is not *Who am I?* but *Who are we?*

CHAPTER 2

HOW WE SEE OURSELVES

Some of us may remember with mild amusement an occasion when larking about with a group of friends we tumbled out of the tight squeeze of a passport-photo booth, laughing and joking, blind to the disapproving glares of passers-by. Minutes earlier we had posed in excited and tense expectation of the flashes of light in the small glass window shielding the camera. To this day the strips of gently fading passport-size photographs remain stuck on the doors of our fridges, immortalised portraits of joyful friendships, gesturing across the huge distances that now separate us.

Whether we are looking at a photograph on our fridge or in a gallery, when we look *beyond the face* in a portrait of a friend or stranger, we are one human being looking at another. Frequently we are looking at faces from another period of time, or another culture or nation, but what we always have in common as human beings proves to be wonderfully fertile soil in which can grow a true sense of wellbeing. This will not only help us to be at peace with ourselves and others but will also combat the fear-driven 'tribalism' infecting and brutalising our world. Before looking more closely at portraits and how artists have employed different devices to help us go *beyond the face*, we shall explore this common soil of our humanity.

The understanding of our humanity upon which this book is based is found in the Judeo-Christian tradition: we are relational human beings with a God-given body and soul. This belief is teased out in the opening chapters of the book of Genesis, in the creation narratives common to the scriptures of Judaism and Christianity. They reveal a profound wisdom in the form of dramatic poetic myth. In the narratives, Adam and Eve (who are human archetypes) become the central characters; God forms their bodies from the dust of the earth at the climax of his creation. God then breathes his spirit into their bodies, and they are 'ensouled', they become living beings with body and soul. God does this because (as Jesus revealed), God is love and love by nature is self-giving. The soul is thus comprised of the spirit of God (which is immutable), and the totality of the mind, will, desires, feelings, and affections, all of which are mutable and which for Adam and Eve swiftly come into play as the narratives develop. The most startling revelation, unique to the creation myths of the ancient religions, is that Adam and Eve are made in the image of God; they bear his likeness. This likeness is most vividly seen in their capacity to love and be loved, and the freedom to reject being loving and loved; for love by its nature must be freely chosen.

In the narratives we see the vigorous creative life of God manifest in life on earth and most particularly in Adam and Eve who are commanded to:

> Be *fruitful and multiply and fill the earth and subdue it; and have dominion over the fish of the sea and over the birds of the air and over every living thing that moves upon the earth.* Genesis 1:28

There is a diversity, harmony and purposefulness expressed here that is perhaps best described in the metaphor of life as a 'dance' – with God taking the lead.

Many artists have worked hard to express and expound the mystery and wonder of being human, with body and soul. In 2005, having been shown in a number of temporary exhibitions, Antony Gormley's *Another Place* (1997) was installed on Crosby beach in Liverpool. It is made up of one-hundred cast-iron, life-size human figures, standing along the foreshore looking out to sea **(Figure 3)**. Gormley writes:

> *In this work human life is tested against planetary time. This sculpture exposes to light and time the nakedness of a particular and peculiar body. It is no hero, no ideal, just the industrially reproduced body of a middle-aged man trying to remain standing and trying to breathe, facing a horizon busy with ships moving materials and manufactured things around the planet. (4)*

Each of Gormley's statues is identical and is cast from a mould of the artist's own body, a mould made at a single point in time. In the juxtaposition of the 'moment' represented by the cast, the 'sequence of moments' in the coming and going of ships and visitors, the 'decades' of the slowly decaying cast-iron and the 'millennia' of planetary tidal-forces, Gormley presents us with a 'slow dance' of time, eternity, and human being. There is something beautifully resonant about the human-like statues, with their soul-like materiality (subject to the elemental forces of decay) and their spirit-like immutability.

The truth expressed in the full scope of the Genesis creation narratives is that within the decay and death that is elemental to life on earth (part of its very renewal and beauty), humankind has a calling to become the best of itself in body and soul, by yielding to the life of God present within (through his spirit). To live thus is to honour God the creator and is the path of wellbeing, of contentment and satisfaction. It is the impulse at the core of this book, taking us *beyond the face*; ours and that of others.

THE FACE OF OUR BODY

In the Genesis narratives, Adam is formed from the dust of the ground and Eve is formed from one of Adam's ribs; we are first and foremost physical beings. We are of course acutely aware of this, after all we are invariably preoccupied with caring for our bodies and either celebrating their vitality or lamenting their frailty. It is often our face that gives a clue to what state we are in, how we are living with our bodies at any moment in time. As passengers on a train or in a lift we are usually among strangers in the faces we see around us, sometimes they catch our eye but mostly we're looking into a screen or lost in the distance. Often the face acts as a mask, especially among strangers, but it also has the capacity to be a window into the state of the body and the inner world of the soul.

At one level our faces are physical structures of skin, bone, tissue, muscle, hair and much more. More than forty muscles animate the human face and humans have developed an extraordinary ability to recognise and read a face – an ability refined from that moment when as baby we latched onto our mother's face, she who we trusted to protect and nourish us. In later years we adorn our faces with make-up or tattoos, we fine-tune our faces with surgery, and we enhance our faces with piercings and other accessories. The colours, textures and wrinkles of our faces offer clues to our heritage and our story. Many of our faces do not fit the norms, they stand out in the crowd, while disfigurement or disability offer clues to unusual stories. The human face is extraordinarily subtle and complex – perfectly fitted to be a window onto the varied landscapes of our souls. When we notice a face in a portrait, or even our own face in a mirror, our sensory neurons immediately fire in all directions, noticing, classifying, making comparisons, and forming opinions. So much goes on 'at first sight' of the face, that invariably judgements and opinions are well wide of the mark and deepen pre-conceptions.

The digital era has rapidly magnified the obsession to define ourselves and others through the look of our faces. 'I am my body' is an infant self-perception that many of us have never left behind, we continue to satisfy a pressing need to protect ourselves by fitting in with those who look like us or promote ourselves with an exceptional face that stands out from the crowd. Often to our detriment, our sense of wellbeing is shaped by the image we have of ourselves in others' eyes. In 1902, the sociologist Charles Horton Cooley wrote:

> *I am not what I think I am, and I am not what you think I am. I am what I think you think I am. (5)*

This will be a precarious state when we are at all ill-at-ease with our assumed image and its preservation will exhaust us. However, in our best moments, when we arise from sleep and can love the face in the mirror, we will be content to be true to ourselves and others around us, to allow our face to reveal something of our inner soul – however beautiful or ugly our face might be deemed to be.

Mercifully the cultural tide is slowly changing and more of us are refusing to submit to the lie that 'I am my body' or that our body ought to conform, lies that dispose us either to adapt our faces to fit in or to stand out. Even toy manufacturers are moving away from body stereotypes. In 2021 Mattel, the makers of the Barbie doll (a young girl's icon of looks), abandoned the blond haired, perfectly contoured face of yesteryear when it released a doll modelled on Professor Sarah Gilbert the co-creator of the Oxford/AstraZeneca COVID-19 vaccine. The boundaries between human bodies of different appearance, ability, race or gender are now much more pervious than even a generation ago.

As we gaze at the face in a portrait, we need to take time to appreciate its physical features and particularities, the physical beauty of a fellow human being like us, lovingly made from the dust of the earth, from the God-given material of life. To do so properly, we will have to make every effort to reject cultural stereotypes of the body.

THE FACE OF OUR SOUL

In the National Trust's stately homes the honoured faces of history, of power and status, gaze down at us from on high. In our churches, faces in stone and stained glass remind us of spiritual teaching that most of us can barely remember. In company lobbies and university receptions faces on the wall leave us in no doubt who is in charge. In government offices hang the familiar face of the monarch and the unfamiliar faces of former public servants. Outside on billboards gargantuan faces sell us the must-have lip-gloss and beard-oil, while in the public square stands an empty plinth where, now toppled from sight, there once stood the proud upright face of a former slave-owner. In our homes faces of loved ones decorate our living spaces, the walls of our teenager's bedroom are splashed with the brash faces of fandom, while in our waking hours the faces of family members, friends, strangers and colleagues are ever present. Faces adorn, they represent, they stir memory, they provoke anger, they inspire virtue, and they hold clues to our inner hidden worlds, worlds more alike than most of us care to consider or dare to imagine. The face is not simply a passive and incidental 'window', it's an indispensable frontier onto the inner world of the soul.

In the creation narratives, Adam and Eve are created from the material of the earth and are animated by the spirit (literally 'breath') of God – they become spiritual beings, distinct from all other living species. The narratives suggest to us that we are all spiritual beings made in the image or likeness of God – for God is spirit. The glorious diversity of humans we see around us is the outworking of this life of God being made present and visible through bodies and souls (the soul comprising spirit, mind, will, desires, feelings, and affections). To be human is to live well whatever our capacitates, to find ourselves strangely satisfied and content within the limits of body and soul. To achieve this, we are invited to yield to the life of God within, God who is love.

However, as we all well know this ideal is nigh impossible to achieve. Our wills, being free in every moment to accept or reject the love of God, dispose us towards love of self. In the creation narratives this reality is illustrated in the temptation of Adam and Eve to eat the forbidden fruit from the tree of the knowledge of good and evil in the middle of the garden. They succumb to this temptation, they sin; rejecting the love of God and giving in to their base desires for autonomy. They prefer to be their own God and, as they say: 'the rest is history'.

The face in a mirror and the face in a portrait are two bodies and souls in which the image or likeness of God has been disfigured by countless poor choices between 'good and evil', choices made by us and by others. Prejudice, spite, and hatred are manifestations of this. But all is not lost, for the immutable spirit within our soul is persistently inviting us (through our will), to yield our mind, our desires, our feelings, and our affections to the love of God. His love can redeem our failures, incorporating the consequences of our poor choices into the rich 'tapestry' of who we and others are. Finding ourselves strangely content and at peace we will say in the words of the ancient hymn: 'all is well with my soul'.

As we look to go *beyond the face* in a portrait, we will become aware of the profound and beautiful complexities of our two lives, for we are embodied beings with souls, each with the capacity to love or to reject love. To truly go *beyond the face* is to accept ourselves as spiritual beings and yield to the love of God which wells up within, through the spirit. To yield in this way is challenging, for the will to autonomy is strong, however the tools of mindfulness, meditation and contemplation introduced in Chapter 4 can assist us in what will prove to be an immensely rewarding and important endeavour.

OUR RELATIONSHIPS

The creation narratives are full of relationships of one kind or another. At the creation of humankind God says:

> *let us make them in our image, according to our likeness.* Genesis 1:26

This is a highly enigmatic description of God; Judaism is a monotheistic religion however this suggests that God is relational within and outside of himself. This desire for relationship with his creatures proves to be a key feature of God's choice to create humankind in his likeness. Eve is created to be a 'helper' for Adam, his equal companion, and the author describes their relationship as the foundation for family and household:

> *therefore, a man leaves his father and mother and clings to his wife, and they become one flesh.* Genesis 2:24

Later we see Adam, Eve, and God all walking in the garden 'at the time of the evening breeze' a beautiful picture of mutual presence and intimacy.

The wisdom of the ancient African concept of Ubuntu proposes that; 'a person is only a person through other people', or put another way, that 'I am what I am because of other people'. We are relational beings. To be open and willing to meet another person through their face in a portrait is to choose to be present to them. It is to venture to find ourselves, to know more of our true selves than we could ever know alone. Our identity is so much more than that which is described by the physicality of our face, our identity arises in the relations of two or more souls to one another. Without other humans (and without God), our capacity to receive and give love has no outlet and we find ourselves alone and diminished. Most of us however, with great effort and ingenuity, have invested our post-childhood years learning to be 'free spirits': the thrill of the world's enticements inclining us to autonomy; we want to be our own God. Martin Luther, the German reformer described this state of affairs as the human soul turned in on itself, into a way of living that proves perversely contrary to the freedom it purports to be. Turned in on ourself, when we meet other people we find that we most naturally relate to others who like us or who are like us. They make us feel safe, they reinforce our sense of who we are, and they are the easiest people to have fun with. If we look at the portraits we have curated on our smartphones, those which adorn our homes or those which most readily catch our eye in the gallery, the vast majority will be of people we like or at least that we like the look of, and they are invariably smiling, happy people. After all nobody in their right mind would hang the scowling face of their arch-enemy in their living room! If we ever bother to pay attention to portraits of those we dislike or distrust it may simply be to make us feel better about ourselves, to affirm us in our self-righteousness.

Choosing not to be our own God, to yield our soul to turn out from itself, towards others and towards God, is the path to self-discovery, to realising our true nature as those who are made for relationships. We will need courage and perseverance to remove the barriers we have erected for ourselves, to get to understand and appreciate those who are very different from us, including those we dislike or hate. To take this path towards another's world will be for a few moments to walk in their shoes and to allow ourselves to be both the observer and the observed. Then, insofar as we find some relationship between us, we will notice the barriers slowly fracture and crumble and we will begin to discover our true self, perhaps for the first time. This way must be travelled in a spirit of humility, noticing the other person without judgement as a fellow human being like us, wonderfully made from dust of the earth, infused with the immutable life of God and loved indiscriminately by him. As the fourteenth-century English mystic Julian of Norwich noted:

> *To love a human being means to accept him as he is, if you wait until he is different you are only loving an idea. (6)*

In empathising with another person in a portrait we may well find ourselves seeing facets of our own soul we'd rather not see. It is not an exercise in self-improvement or to salve our conscience, it is motivated by a sense, however fragile, that this other person is just like us, complex, gifted, and equally marred by poor choices and the buffeting of a harsh world. Empathy in this place of pain draws out compassion, which is literally to 'suffer-with'. Henri Nouwen was a Dutch Roman Catholic priest, professor and writer who spent many years working alongside adults with learning and other developmental disabilities. He writes:

> *Compassion is born when we discover in the centre of our own existence not only that God is God and man is man, but also that our neighbour is really our fellow man … through compassion it is possible to recognise that the cravings for love that men feel reside also in our own hearts, that the cruelty that the world knows all too well is also rooted in our own impulses. (7)*

If we do not like what we see of ourselves on this path of self-discovery, then our response will be either to turn back in on ourselves in self-preservation (which may for a while be necessary), or it will be a continuing and courageous turning towards the other and God.

In Judith Kerr's enchanting children's book, *The Tiger Who Came to Tea* (1968), Sophie and her mother welcome into their home a strange tiger who knocks at the door and asks to come to tea. He eats all the food generously offered him, eating them 'out of house and home' and then happily goes on his way. When Sophie's father comes home from work his solution to the complete lack of food in the house is to take the family out for a meal at a café. The following day Sophie's mum buys some tiger food in case their new friend turns up again. In Kerr's story, faced with discomfort and threat, Sophie and her mother adopt a disposition of acceptance and vulnerability towards the unwelcome stranger, and everyone is a winner. Invisible barriers of fear and prejudice crumble away and through courage, imagination, and humility, all is well. The face we notice in a portrait may not be as threatening as a tiger at our door, but the point is well made – we can choose to ignore it or we can choose to embrace it with loving attention.

CONCLUSION

The Psalmist in the Judeo-Christian book of the Psalms describes human beings as 'fearfully and wonderfully made'. Created in God's image, we have extraordinary bodies and souls with the ability (with God's help), to become the best of ourselves. As we become more fully present and reconciled to ourselves and to one another we will discover a wellbeing and contentment not contingent on circumstance. This is not a straightforward path to take. It will challenge us because it is counter-cultural when the world is so obsessed with the condition of the body and inclines us to relate only to others like us (made in our own image). However, if we're able to play our small part by going *beyond the face*, we will make the world a kinder, more hospitable, and forgiving place, and so the struggle will have been worthwhile.

CHAPTER 3
HOW PORTRAITS WORK

A portrait is a work of art with an intimate and thoughtful history. Even the portraits on the coins and notes in our pockets have their own long and complex history as tokens of value, identity, and authenticity.

The style or manner of a portrait is established early on in its evolution and will reflect the portrait's purpose in the mind of the artist and, if it's the case, the mind of the person paying for its commission. The purpose of a portrait might be:

- To capture a memory of the subject.

- To give a stamp of authority or an air of prestige to the subject (e.g. for a national collection or a royal commission).

- As an aid to prayer (e.g. a religious Icon).

- To evoke feeling and intimate connection (e.g. for a jewellery locket or for a domestic setting).

- To probe the inner worlds of the subconscious mind (e.g. surrealist portraits).

- To subvert a cultural stereotype (e.g. portraits in the Brit. Art of the 1980s and in the LGBTQ+ community in the twenty-first century).

- To caricature someone in the public eye (e.g. a political cartoon).

- To reconcile self-image (e.g. an intimate self-portrait).

The artist may be a professional of some renown or they may be an enthusiastic amateur. They may paint, draw, or sculpt their subject at multiple live sittings, from a photograph, or from memory or imagination. They might be constrained by the brief given to them or they may have the joy (or terror) of complete free rein. Limits and freedoms will affect both the offer made to the artist by the subject and the creative choices of the artist. There are a vast array of choices to be made: of size and proportion, perspective, posture, background, accessories, fidelity to likeness or persona, appearance in present time or past, flattery or reality, media, materials and even the choice of title. Many choices are made either at the click of a camera shutter or in a process of negotiation and experimentation over a much longer period. It's important that in 'looking to notice' during Step 1 of the method in Chapter 5, the options chosen and declined are regarded.

Portraiture is a demanding genre; it is fitting that we should honour the work of the artist and the life of the subject by paying close attention to their work; approaching the portrait with humility and in a spirit of hopeful encounter. First, we shall consider the qualities of a portrait and how artists have intentionally or unintentionally paved the way for us to go *beyond the face*.

QUALITIES OF A PORTRAIT

1. Likeness

When we look at a portrait we instinctively consider some aspect or degree of physical likeness to the subject (whether we know them or not), as if demand for physical realism is a primary force in the process of looking. However, if the style or manner of the portrait is obviously allegorical or metaphorical, we are likely to suspend this quest in favour of a search for truth in meaning rather than accuracy of representation. The image of Jesus the Good Shepherd **(Figure 4)** is a metaphorical reference to the way he guides and protects those who listen to his voice. In this instance the portrait is rich in reinforcing symbolism; the shepherd's guiding staff, the cradled sheep, the cross of sacrifice, the trinitarian trefoil and the banner inscription, 'I know my sheep'.

In the choices facing the portrait artist who sets out to represent a likeness, decisions are largely aesthetic. Questions of taste, convention and perceptions of beauty reverberate in the mind and world of the artist, subject, commission, and context. Their perceived resolution in a particular portrait is one that needs to be explored in the mind of the observer if a genuine encounter with the subject is desired.

Many portrait artists have been influenced by culturally accepted and idealised views of beauty, most especially in the art of the Italian renaissance of the fourteenth and fifteenth centuries. Portrayals of ideal beauty in the human figure drew on images and ideas from classical antiquity and detailed study of human anatomy. In other generations artists have chosen to accurately represent or even to magnify non-ideal physical characteristics such as shortness, stoutness, blemishes on the skin or defects of limbs; to lead the observer's eye to the subject's quality of mind or soul. It's important to acknowledge that portraits are what they are in every genre and generation. The critical observer needs also to notice their own predilections towards value judgements about beauty, whether exterior or interior, and be ready to challenge themselves if they are to get anywhere near a true encounter with the subject.

Even the exact physical likeness of a face captured in a candid photograph, or a hyperrealist painting begs the question of whether there is more to the face beyond the likeness. Apart from physical likeness there is the likeness of identity; embracing personality, gender, race, sexuality, age, status and more, all that constitutes the soul of the person behind their external features. We can never make a truly objective assessment of likeness of identity; however it behoves us to be receptive to that which the artist and subject are offering in a portrait.

If the relationship between the artist and subject is at all intimate or unduly distorted by the commercial transaction, the likeness will be shaded to some degree by sentimentality and/or flattery. Identity is always formed in relations with others, so sentimentality is likely to skew the likeness where the artist is over-invested emotionally and flattery is likely to skew the likeness if the artist is over-concerned about how the portrait will be received, or if convention demands obedience to type. In her later years artists for Queen Elizabeth I often flattered her by painting her with a face that reflected a more youthful Elizabeth. That said, some degree of emotional investment by both parties *is* necessary if the final portrait is to be worthy of any consideration beyond its external features. Rembrandt van Rijn is an exemplary exponent of such investment, in his sketches and paintings of his mother **(Figure 5)**. Theirs was an era when signs of old age implied stature and wisdom, and matriarchal authority denoted gravitas and stability in the domestic setting.

In all questions of likeness, both to external features and to identity, provisional judgements may well prove helpful provided they remain provisional and open to testing and revision in the process of noticing, responding, and reflecting in the method explained in Chapter 5.

2. Context

Apart from questions of likeness, the portrait artist must make choices in relation to their cultural and artistic context, sometimes in sympathy with prevailing expectations, sometimes in reaction. Cultural conventions create force-fields which artists have to navigate. A primary choice made by the artist is where to position the portrait on the spectrum of possibility between likeness and type; between representing an individual as they are or as prescribed by their role or social status.

The protestant reformation in Northern Europe weakened attachment to social convention and shifted the focus to individual personal identity and freedom. In portraiture this was marked by a gradual shift towards representations which were more focussed on likeness of identity, and which demonstrated a greater self-consciousness of personality and character in the 'offer' made by the subject to the artist. Evidence of this is also seen in the growth of self-portraiture from the seventeenth century onwards, Rembrandt van Rijn painted eighty self-portraits over a period of more than thirty years, giving us a very personal record of his changing looks and character.

In the nineteenth century, following the decline of the nobility and landed gentry and the rise of the middle classes, increasing numbers of the latter re-enforced their place in society through commissioned portraits in which dress, setting and insignia broadcast their position in the social hierarchy. The inclusion of servants and tradespeople of lower rank in the portrait further reinforced status and authority, as did any choice to seat the subject on horseback or to paint their portrait in a full-frontal pose.

As the nineteenth century drew to a close, the avant-garde mounted a challenge to both the dominance of the academies and the rise of photography by opening up new frontiers: Impressionism, Expressionism, Surrealism, Dada and so forth. These were movements that in their portraiture firmly established the life *beyond the face* as worthy of exploration and expression, where the soul became a dominant influence.

In the later twentieth century, John Berger's seminal work *Ways of Seeing* (Penguin Modern Classics, 2008) was a powerful exposé of the visual landscape of modern Western consumerism, illustrating how historic forces of misogyny, privilege and wealth had almost indelibly influenced the affectations of both artists and consumers. However cultural and social awareness was turning the tide, and this was reflected in many spheres including portraiture. West comments on the shifting nature of this landscape in relation to gender:

The representation of masculinity and its manifestations had become much more self-conscious in recent portraiture, especially among some gay artists – what has changed in the representation of masculinity between the sixteenth and late twentieth centuries is the degree of self-consciousness in the treatment of masculinity and male identity. (8)

The British artist Jenny Saville is particularly well known for her striking portraits of mostly unnamed 'types' of large nude women in which she discloses the narrative of the human body as it is. Saville mounts a brazen confrontation with marketplace images of idealised womanly beauty which have been codified in commercial art and marketing and have become the curse of teenage identity angst. It's a tribute to the work of Saville and others that marketing trends today evidence a growing penchant for body shapes and facial features more representative of the population, superseding vain idealisations.

Perhaps now more than ever, portraits in the public sphere have become objects that both reflect and challenge prevailing cultural norms and perceptions. Commercialised faces and celebrity icons jostle with faces of ordinary heroes and under-represented minorities. These are all inescapable features of the modern cultural context in which the portrait artist is working. They do so more or less self-consciously; the reality is that all of us, artists and observers, are products of the same landscape.

Personal identity is one of the most pressing issues for post-modern people. Identity authentication, individual rights of expression and concealment of the face for protection from respiratory viruses have conspired to give unprecedented focus upon the human face. There is a pressing urgency for us to address the question of who we and who others are, in the context of today's cultural forces – embracing both the face and the person *beyond the face.* 'Virtue signalling' is no new phenomenon, however the complexities of this conscientised and uber-connected world mean that that it takes an unusual level of effort to read a portrait in order to truly see the subject. It's an effort which provides rich rewards for those willing to stay the course; enriched and reconciled human relations are always worth striving for.

The relationship between an artist and a patron has a subtle influence on the dynamics of a portrait. The artist *may* have free rein; however many commercial portraits are the product of a series of transactions with their patron so it's possible that the artist may consider themselves constrained if the brief is too restrictive or the relationship with the patron affected. Established in 1856, the original aspirations of the National Portrait Gallery (NPG) in London were to celebrate significant and prominent national figures, mostly statesmen and men of distinction in the world of the arts. The very notion of significance is a value judgement for gallery and artist; the artist's task was to manifest and celebrate the chosen subject's significance using devices with both cultural resonance and public appeal.

However, in this post-modern world, one of the principal purposes of the NPG is now:

To promote through the medium of portraits the appreciation and understanding of the men and women who have made and are making British history and culture. (9)

This reflects a recognition that national institutions are not simply curators of cultural and social history but play a significant part in shaping a nation's self-understanding. NPG briefings for commissioned artists provide clear guidance which helps shape their creative endeavour. The example portraits from the NPG discussed in Chapter 6 reflect this new reality.

Other contextual factors in the making of a portrait may be of a more incidental nature. For example, the invention of the flat mirror in seventeenth-century Europe elevated the artist into the higher echelons of society as self-portraiture afforded a vehicle for self-promotion. In contrast, it is widely accepted that one of the factors leading to Van Gogh's numerous self-portraits is that he could either ill-afford models or his reputation for unpredictable behaviour repelled possible contenders. We have the good fortune of being in possession of a significant quantity of Van Gogh's personal correspondence; often this gives an insight into his inner and outer worlds, helping us understand the inner dynamics of both his self-portraits and portraits.

It's sometimes said that a good photographic portrait is not taken it is given, an observation which applies to all portraiture. What the subject gives to the artist will be a more or less self-conscious offering of body and soul, an offering which is always made within the context of their relationship. Questions of vanity and affectation are vitally important when teasing out the nature of this offering, especially in eras when portraits were the preserve of the wealthy and powerful or those seeking to make a name for themselves. These subtle social and cultural forces influencing the features of a portrait make this a complex journey of discovery.

3. Presence

Taken at face-value a portrait represents the subject in two or three static dimensions, at a fixed point in time. It is often an image made in one context then displayed in another and perhaps reproduced many times over for very diverse markets. It is remarkable, for example, how Frida Kahlo's self-portrait has made its way from gallery to guidebook to T-shirt **(Figure 6)** and even onto a pencil case and into a screen-saver!

Beyond a portrait's face-value is its 'presence', an intimation arising out of the proximity of two human souls (those of subject and observer), without constraint of time or space. This presence makes deeper and more intimate engagement possible, one that goes well beyond face-value. A spiritual encounter is possible if we are willing to contemplate for a while.

It is this understanding of presence that for Christian believers underpins the use of religious Icons in the discipline of prayer. The iconographer, using a stylised and codified form of painting, creates an imagined portrait of a Saint of the church or of Jesus Christ, as an act of prayer itself. The Icon then acts a window through which the believer has access to the invisible realm of these transfigured Saints. In uniting with their 'presence' the believer's worship is absorbed into the worship of heaven. This way of seeing arises out of a belief in the 'communion of Saints': the interconnectedness of souls, living and departed, mediated by the Spirit of God. This magnifying of a 'presence' in heaven to a worshipper on earth through an Icon requires an artistic work with an extraordinarily tender and humble touch, one that is made possible by the discipline of a community of prayer.

Symbols are used by artists to magnify some aspect of the subject's life or work, to add gravitas to their presence. In many traditional Icons of the Virgin Mary, three stars on Mary's veil signify her virginity before, during and after the conception of Christ (according to the doctrine of perpetual virginity) **(Figure 9)**. Her presence as this mother-without-sin is magnified by the symbolic device. Furthermore, her temporal presence in the Icon is softened by a halo adorning a serene face and a robe of transcendent blue, signifying an eternal and heavenly presence. The Christian believer, praying before the Icon, is transported *beyond the faces* of Mary and her son, into communion with the Spirit of God; who unites all who live in humble obedience to the will of God.

In Hans Holbein the Younger's *The Ambassadors* **(Figure 7)**, Holbein uses objects to magnify the presence of the subjects in an intensely rich treatise on sixteenth-century relations between England and France. The faces of the two ambassadors are almost incidental to the whole which gains its force through a panoply of objects full of symbolic meaning. These objects signify scientific endeavour, political allegiance, ecclesiastical disharmony, conquest, mortality and more. The presence of the two men is magnified by the objects and symbols of their trades and professions.

Imaginative abstraction is device whereby portrait artists dissolve form to evoke a sensibility to an identity of presence rather than likeness of form. Pablo Picasso, Paul Klee and Katherine Dreier use line, shape, curves, and colours in their portraits to render biographical detail virtually irrelevant and to elicit instead a stillness of presence which inclines towards type, the simple stripped-back type of human 'being'. Francis Bacon's semi-abstract portraits and self-portraits often expose the intensely carnal nature of this human 'being'. Raw and fleshy, they are images which the observer may behold, noticing their own visceral reactions as one embodied human being in the presence of another **(Figure 2)**.

Dress is a device frequently deployed by artists to magnify the presence of their subject. The medals pinned to the uniform of Lance Corporal Gideon Beharry VC, in his portrait in the National Portrait Gallery, include his Victoria Cross **(Figure 15)**. The casual observer may have no prior knowledge of this soldier or his life of service, or of the significance of this particular medal. However, it is clear at first sight that this is a soldier being commended for serving his country – his medals and uniform magnify his presence. Other forms of dress amplify the presence of the subject of a portrait through identification with their role or status. Historically, monarchs, bishops, captains of industry, judges and university vice-chancellors have been attired for their portraits in a manner befitting their position in the hierarchy of their institution. Whether the stature of their presence in the portrait is commensurate with reality is a moot point – one worthy of exploration in Step 3 (response), of the method in Chapter 5. In contrast the executives of contemporary companies with a strong brand image (e.g. Apple, Microsoft and Facebook) are more likely to 'dress down' for their portrait, choosing to dispense with the iconic and symbolic uniforms of yesteryear, to communicate a presence which is more informal and on a par with their target audience.

Iconic self-portraits are often regarded for their psychological presence, exposing the true self *beyond the face*: a visual window to the soul. This may be a tortured soul, one seeking relief or liberation in self-expression. Van Gogh painted over thirty-five self-portraits in his lifetime, demonstrating his versatility as an artist and leaving an intimate autobiographical record. Those he painted in the last three years of his life (as he wrestled with mental illness, self-isolation, and disappointment), provide a sobering and powerful insight into the vicissitudes of his mind. In Van Gogh's *Self-portrait with a Bandaged Ear* (1889) and *Raising of*

Lazarus (1890), in which he models the face of Lazarus upon himself), Van Gogh is powerfully present, as if mental anguish has temporarily erased all affectation and pretence. Likewise, the self-portraits of Mexican surrealist artist Frida Kahlo are boldly candid in their depiction of the chronic pain she endured following childhood polio and a bus accident in her late teens. Her *Broken Column* **(Figure 8)** has an extraordinarily powerful psychological presence constituted by her semi-naked, dissected, nailed and scaffolded body in a barren landscape. With even scant biographical knowledge an observer of any of these three self-portraits would be hard pressed to resist a sense of psychological presence commanding curiosity and respect. The prevalence of mental illness and chronic pain in Western societies is well documented; the three-step method affords artists like Van Gogh and Frida Kahlo, who have bared their souls, the opportunity to invite observers to surrender themselves to the stark reality of the human condition, to find relief and consolation in human relations.

Portraits are placed in public spaces to influence the collective psyche. They make the subject's presence felt, re-enforce expectations and promote fealty. Examples include images of a head of state in a school classroom, civic building or public square. Adolf Hitler used his portrait as propaganda, promoting patriotism among the German people and stamping the authority of Nazi ideology upon the collective psyche. The medium was the message: the supremacy of the Aryan race. The toppling of the statue of Saddam Hussein by American Forces in Baghdad in 2003 became almost mythical in the eyes of the Western press. The ability of such acts of violence to effect a loosening of decades of repression in the Iraqi psyche (and to reinforce Western self-righteousness), bears witness to the subliminal power of a portrait's presence in a public space.

ARTISTIC DEVICES IN A PORTRAIT

In the history of the genre, artists have deployed a variety of devices to help the observer to look *beyond the face*. In order to properly notice the soul of the subject it is helpful to understand how these devices are intended to work in order to be able to work with them in a spirit of cooperative discovery. The following examples are not exhaustive but serve to arouse interest and closer attention.

1. Grammar – Schools of Iconography

Religious Icons have a grammar, they work within a set of rules – which are understood by both the iconographer and observer (or more accurately, worshipper). Different 'schools' of iconography have their own subtle distinctions of grammar which have arisen in distinct cultural contexts. An Icon is not intended to elicit an emotional response in the observer, subjects are rarely shown with facial expression and they are always painted with closed mouths. Icons are without shadow, the light upon the subject comes from within, creating a luminescence which engenders a still presence. In **Figure 9** Jesus is both a child and an adult and the Greek letters ὸ ω ν written into his halo are the equivalent of the Hebrew YHWH, which means 'I am': Jesus is eternal, unconstrained by human time.

Perspective in the Icon is often reversed: the worshipper has a sense of being observed by the subject, drawn into a liminal space between material and immaterial worlds. Symbols, colours, words, and letters have their own grammatical significance, to be fleetingly noticed by the knowledgeable worshipper.

The grammar skill and prayerful disposition of the iconographer and the discipline of the worshipper combine to make the subject of the Icon 'present', to close the space between them, transporting them into the world of the transcendent *beyond the face,* souls in communion.

2. Colouration – Vincent van Gogh

Van Gogh began to experiment with colour in 1887, during his first year in Paris. Though he had previously studied the use of colour by the Dutch masters, it was in Paris that Van Gogh became a serious collector of Japanese art with its large flat areas of colour. His interest in this art went beyond aesthetic appreciation after he moved to Arles, projecting onto Provence his emerging vision of Japan as a paradise of colour and beauty. There he quickly developed his own bright and colourful palette, one that became a cornerstone of his painting. In referring to the blue sky of Provence, the limpid air and the brilliance of the orange, yellow and red flowers he notes:

> *There's something happier and more suggestive of love than in the north. It vibrates like the bouquet by Monticelli that you have. (10) 8th August 1888*

Van Gogh based his use of colour on the theories of the nineteenth-century French Romantic artist, Eugene Delacroix who sought to 'excite' the eye of the observer using colours in proximity rather than blended. Van Gogh juxtaposed primary and complementary colours to increase the brilliance: blue against orange, red against green and yellow against violet. This was his reference point when he wrote:

In a painting I'd like to say something consoling, like a piece of music. I'd like to paint men or women with that je ne sais quoi of the eternal, of which the halo used to be the symbol, and which we try to achieve through the radiance itself, through the vibrancy of our colorations. (11) 3rd September 1888

Over a three-month period in Arles, during which he suffered mental anguish, disappointment, rejection and loneliness, Van Gogh painted five almost identical portraits of Augustine Roulin (who had become his surrogate mother in Arles). Each titled *La Berceuse* **(Figure 10)**, which can be translated as cradle song or lullaby, Van Gogh used complementary colours to paint a portrait that is powerfully Icon-like and imbued with his own yearning for consolation.

In *The Night Café* (1888) Van Gogh used reds and greens to embody what he described as the terrible human passions and when living in the asylum at St Remy he tells fellow artist Emile Bernard how he uses colour to describe:

The feelings of anxiety from which some of my companions in misfortune suffer. (12) 26th November 1889

In contrast to the symbolic use of colour in religious Icons, Van Gogh used colour to energise his portraits, to excite the sight and imagination of the observer. His intent was to draw the observer beyond the surface and vibrancy of the colours to that which lay beyond, to the soul of his subjects.

2. Imagination and symbol – René Magritte and Leonora Carrington

Surrealism was a movement arising out of the deep shadows of the first world war, a response to the failure of enlightenment optimism which had elevated man in the hierarchy of being and which had elevated rationalism. Surrealism sought to reunite the worlds of the conscious and the unconscious, to discover that which was above and beyond reality. Poets and painters were said to have a privileged access to this sur-reality, drawing heavily from the world of dreams, fantasy, and symbol, juxtaposing the fantastical with the mythical and the everyday, using tactics designed to awaken the observer from their desolate complacency.

Portraiture was not especially dominant in surrealism, however one iconic example is the self-portrait by Belgian artist René Magritte, *Son of Man* **(Figure 11)**. Commissioned by his friend and patron Harry Torczyner, Magritte admitted he found difficulty with painting his own portrait as a 'problem of conscience'; the very notion that an artist could represent themselves was an anathema within the surrealist movement. Magritte said of his painting:

> *Everything we see hides another thing, we always want to see what is hidden by what we see, but it is impossible. Humans hide their secrets too well … There is an interest in that which is hidden and which the visible does not show us. This interest can take the form of a quite intense feeling, a sort of conflict, one might say, between the visible that is hidden and the visible that is present. (13)*

Magritte invites the observer to consider the everyday reality that lies about them, even the notion of reality itself, suspending judgement regarding what really *is* or *is not*. The motif of the man in a suit with a bowler hat (the way Magritte himself mostly dressed), renders that which is unremarkable and everyday. The apple obscuring most of the face gives a brazen immediacy to this play between what is visible and hidden and visible and present. The eyes, the windows to the soul, can just be seen, but identity is obscured. This is an 'in your face' attempt to encourage the observer to go *beyond the face.*

Magritte rejected the idea of religious meaning, however it would be consistent with his desire to probe the subconscious to acknowledge that his chosen title *Son of Man* is one of the names claimed by Jesus to reference his twin natures, and that the apple is symbolic of the human temptation to become our own god. Perhaps the faceless businessman in his grey suit and bowler hat is a trope of conformity to the norm, a *Son of Man* who is 'everyman' – we are hiding our divine image in favour of the self-interested obsessions of our human nature.

A more fantastical self-portrait is that by the surrealist English artist Leonora Carrington, *Self-Portrait, Inn of the Dawn Horse* (1938). Carrington places herself in the corner of a room beneath a white rocking horse and facing a lactating hyena. In the far wall of the room is an open window making visible a galloping white horse. Horses are common in Carrington's work (signifying liberty), and a rocking horse above Carrington is probably a reference to a play she's written about a young girl who is in love with her rocking horse. Carrington with her shock of hair and the wild fecund hyena (with which she said she identified), both look outwards towards the observer. In a BBC documentary featuring the work of Leonora Carrington the narrator makes the point that:

The subconscious has a syntactic language that is truly a universal language for it does not depend on education or culture or intelligence but speaks with the vocabulary of the great vital constants, sexual instincts, awareness of death, sense of the mystery of space – these vital constants are universally echoed in every human being. (14)

This is what makes surrealist portraits a fascinating and rich resource for tapping into the world *beyond the face,* less affected as they are by personality and biography, working with resonances in a psycho-spiritual world.

3. Multiple Faces – Lucian Freud and Stanley Spencer

We tend to think of portraits as comprising a single figure, however, artists have deployed multiple figures in relationship to go *beyond the face.* If identity is formed in relation to others, it is perhaps surprising that more isn't made of this device. In Lucian Freud's self-portrait *Reflection with Two Children* (1965) (a reflection in a mirror on the floor), Freud intensifies his presence through a highly oblique angle of view and an off-centre halo-like ceiling light. The combined compositional effect is an upward gravitational pull of the observer into the towering, embodied presence of the figure behind the face. By introducing (with dwarf-like proportions), two of his four children, what might otherwise have been only himself as a man becomes himself as a father, a father removed and distant from his children.

Freud's self-portrait *Hotel Bedroom* (1954), features a woman in bed, hand on her cheek, gazing disconsolately into the distance. Freud paints himself standing behind her (silhouetted in the gloom), with an empty bedroom in the distant background of the window; a portent of their future. The woman is the Guinness heiress, Lady Caroline Hamilton-Temple-Blackwood, with whom Freud eloped after divorcing his first wife. The intensified feelings in the painting reflect a foreboding in their already fraught relationship, a relationship which ended soon after. Freud describes his desire to go beyond representation to feeling:

My object in painting pictures is to try and move the senses by giving an intensification of reality. Whether this can be achieved depends on how intensely the painter understands and feels for the person or object of his choice … the painter makes real to others the innermost feelings about all that he cares for. A secret becomes known to everyone who views the picture through the intensity with which it is felt. (15)

Stanley Spencer's *Portrait of Mr and Mrs Baggett* (1957) was commissioned as separate portraits of the two. However Spencer chose to paint them together in the intimate setting of their Highgate home with the local school and churchyard visible through the half-curtained window, suggesting the long arc of a reality beyond the ordinary. For Spencer the everyday was not ordinary but imbued with the extraordinary; he was intensely concerned with the physical and spiritual impact of 'things' upon the senses. He paints the detail of a phone, a ball of wool, pearls and knitting with the same intense sense of presence as he captures in the faces of Mr and Mrs Baggett:

> *Certainly, things and places seemed to him to possess a double identity, corresponding both to this world and another, heavenly world. He worried when he could not access this other world, when he could not see things in their heavenly aspect. His paintings are an attempt to demonstrate the existence of the double life of things; in a sense they are lessons in seeing. (16)*

A striking feature of the portrait is the contrast between Mrs Baggett who is face-on to the observer and Mr Baggett who is side-on, the latter in the shadows and the former in the light of the window. One has a felt presence, the other a reluctant presence. We know very little about Mr and Mrs Baggett, but we know that Spencer himself had had two unhappy marriages and domestic bliss escaped him. His second wife Patricia Preece had refused to divorce him, wishing to become Lady Spencer when he received his knighthood two years after he painted this portrait. Amanda Bradley comments:

> *Spencer had wanted two wives, the spiritual support from Hilda and carefree excitement from Patricia, but effectively ended up with none. Spencer's aching sense of loss and confusion is evident in his unique evocation of the frailty of human condition. (17)*

4. Absence – Tracey Emin and Mark Quinn

Is a portrait a portrait if it does not contain a face? A work of art may be in the nature of portrait though it might technically defy that definition. The subject's presence may be magnified by their absence through the narrative clues proffered.

British artist Tracey Emin's *My Bed* **(Figure 12)** is one example, an installation created without intent but after the fact: the furniture, furnishings and detritus of a four day alcoholic binge in a period of her life marked by phases of chaos and depression:

It's like a time capsule of my life .... condoms, contraceptive pills, cigarettes, vodka, stains, tiny underwear, all these things are to do with being a girl, coming through a time of transition coming through some cathartic state. (18)

Portraits communicate the subject's identity at a point in time and in a given context. Here, through the tension of absence and presence, Emin's bed discloses someone struggling to come to terms with an emerging identity, confused and battered by forces within and without.

Emin's *My Bed* is reminiscent of Van Gogh's *Bedroom in Arles* (1888), a scene he painted three times in the last two years of his life as he struggled with the impact of frustrated ambition, loneliness and poor mental health. Van Gogh's bedroom was emblematic of a place of rest and contentment, both of which eluded him. Again, technically it's not a portrait but in the tension of absence and presence the observer witnesses the artist's yearning to find their true (spiritual) home: it is a snapshot of their life no less portrait-like than if Van Gogh had painted a self-portrait titled '*Yearning*'.

Mark Quinn's portrait of Nobel Prize-winning scientist *Sir John Sulston* (2001) is entirely abstract. Sulston was a central figure in the development of DNA analysis and interpretation and directed the British contribution to the international Human Genome Project. If a portrait is all about identity, Quinn's portrait which is derived from Sulston's DNA, is just that. Using laboratory procedures to sequence and read DNA, the portrait is simply a plate of agar jelly-covered bacteria colonies that contains random segments of Sulston's genome.

Though abstract, what's remarkable about the portrait is its literalism. Fundamental to our sense of who we are is our appearance, the visible imprint of our DNA. However, DNA is so much more than how we look; it is also about desires, appetites, and probable responses to stimuli. Furthermore, the science of epigenetics (by which environmental and social factors cause certain genes to be switched on or off), reminds us that Sulston's identity is full of possibility. Perhaps Quinn's portrait is closer to a traditional portrait than appears at first glance, we may not see what we expect to see but seeing with an imaginative sensibility to the science enables us to 'see' Sulston in other ways. Quinn said of his DNA portraits:

> *They are like a tunnel through time. They are the ultimate ancestral portrait, as they contain parts of the genome of everyone you are related to, back to the beginning of life. I remember going to the BBC to do*

an interview with John on 11 September 2001, just as the news came through of the planes hitting the Twin Towers. It seemed to both of us on that day and since then that it's similarity between people that is so much more important than the differences between them. To me that's one of the important things these works are about. (19)

The fact that we have 99.9 per cent of our DNA in common with other humans and 98.8 per cent in common with chimpanzees (our closest animal relative), challenges notions of individual achievement, entitlement, and privilege. Quinn helps us think more critically about our ancestral inheritance (and legacy) and about ourselves as intimately interconnected beings.

5. Other Portrait Devices

A search of the archives of the NPG reveals a variety of other artistic devices which take the observer beyond a subject's face, a few of which are highlighted here to further whet the appetite.

In her portrait of the Chief Medical Officer (CMO) *Dame Sally Davis* (2016), Daphne Todd uses three differentiated sections to show various aspects of Davis' role. One section includes her staff in the team office, another the fixtures of her private and personal working world (including an official briefcase and an open bag of fruit), while a third more personal segment includes a prominent ring on her hand and her running shoes. Todd also replicates Davis's eyes three times to signify her different moods: a quiet authority, thoughtful and wearied. These devices intensify Davis's stature in the portrait.

In her 2020 portrait of British tennis player Andy Murray (double Wimbledon winner and Olympic gold medallist), Maggi Hambling employs Murray's energetic movement on the tennis court as her motif, this being emblematic for Murray as he's known by the public. In a single portrait Hambling depicts Murray in four different states of 'full-flight' around the court, together with one traditional face-on pose.

In his 2018 portrait of Malala Yousafzai **(Figure 16)**, artist Shirin Neshat overlays a hand-written text onto her face. Malala rose to prominence in the public eye as an Afghan human rights activist for female education and the text is a poem by the Pashto poet Rahmat Shah Sayel. The subject of the poem is Malala's namesake, Malala of Maiwand – a national hero of Afghanistan who galvanized fighters against British colonial forces in 1880. Neshat uses the text on the portrait as a device to promote a resonance between these two national heroes. This portrait is explored in detail in Chapter 6.

Hyperrealism is a device used by portrait artists to painstakingly represent the texture of their subject's face in intimate detail, suggesting a reality which lies beyond representation. Only at a second glance does the observer realise the portrait is not a photograph, the hyperreality emphasising human physicality and the sensations of the flesh. These portraits undermine initial reactions, getting under the skin of false presumption.

CONCLUSION

Qualities of portraiture are forever morphing under the impact of cultural and other forces while artistic imagination and technical developments have led to the employment of a whole variety of devices to take us *beyond the face.* West says of portraits, that they have become:

> *A method for artists to explore self-consciously, issues of gender, ethnicity, sexuality, and the body. With globalization, the expansion of media, and the co-existence of old and new functions, portraiture at the beginning of the twenty-first century has become a genre of art that has more versatile representational possibilities and functions than ever before. (20)*

These possibilities and functions make the process of truly noticing the subject of a portrait a rich experience, giving us a great deal to work with in Step 1 of the method in Chapter 5. Furthermore, digital media offers a vast library of resources to help the observer understand the artist, context, subject and style of a portrait for Step 2 (responding). However, what is perhaps most difficult in the method is noticing ourselves (as the one doing the noticing), to be attuned to that which inclines us this way or that.

Experience with religious Icons has proved they are most helpful if approached with a prayerful or reflective disposition by which we are able to notice ourselves as the one being observed by the subject. Mindfulness, meditation, and contemplation support this approach and enable us to still ourselves so as to be more truly present to that which is present to us in the face in a portrait. It is to these we now turn before exploring in Chapter 5 how any portrait can function in an Icon-like way, to bring ourselves and the subject together in meaningful encounter.

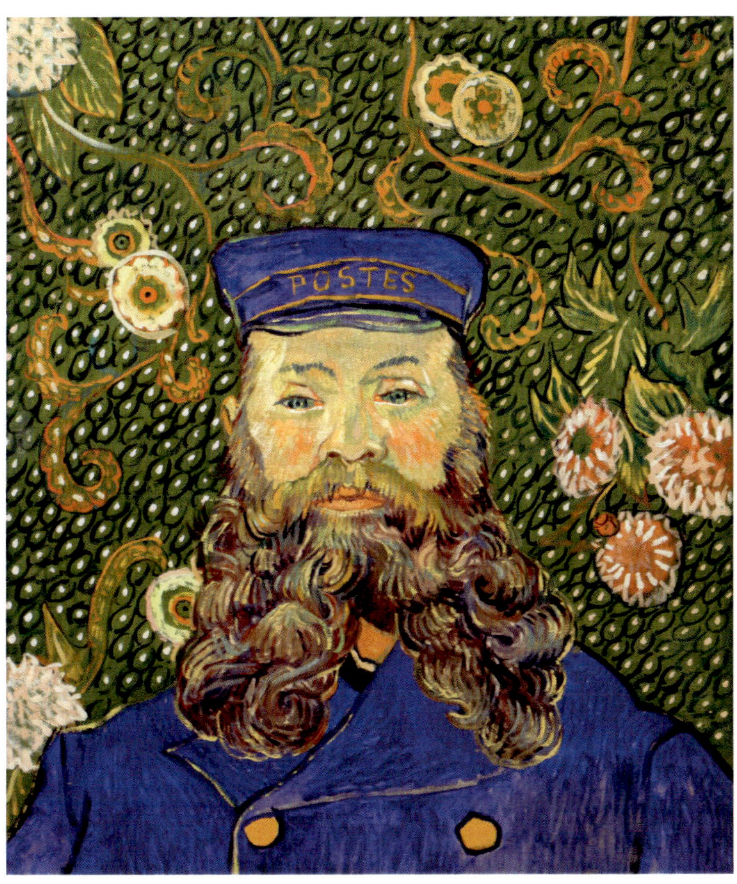

Figure 1: Vincent van Gogh, *Portrait of the Postman Joseph Roulin (1888)*, Museum of Modern Art, New York. Image, Peter Barritt, Alamy.

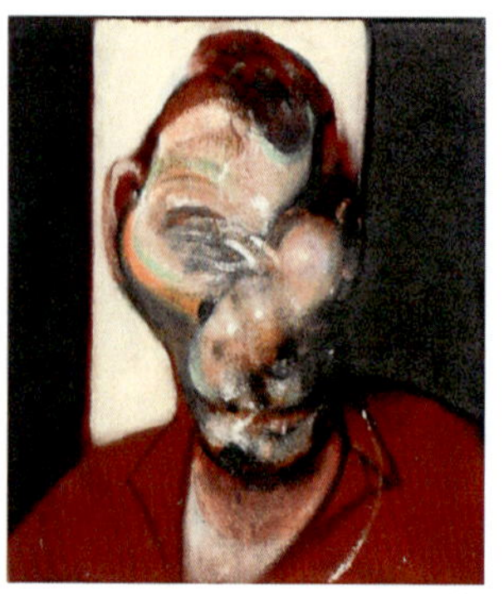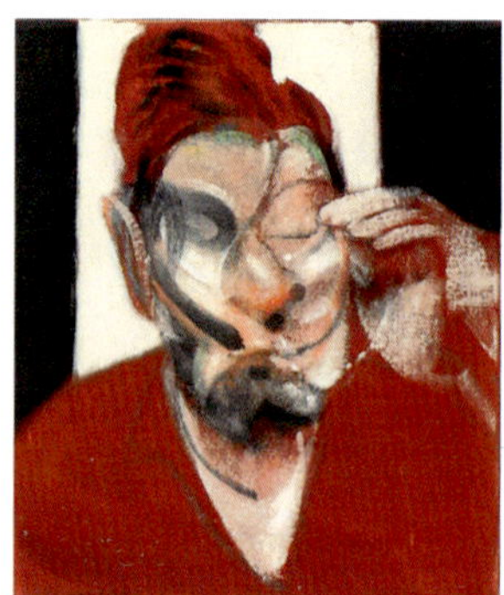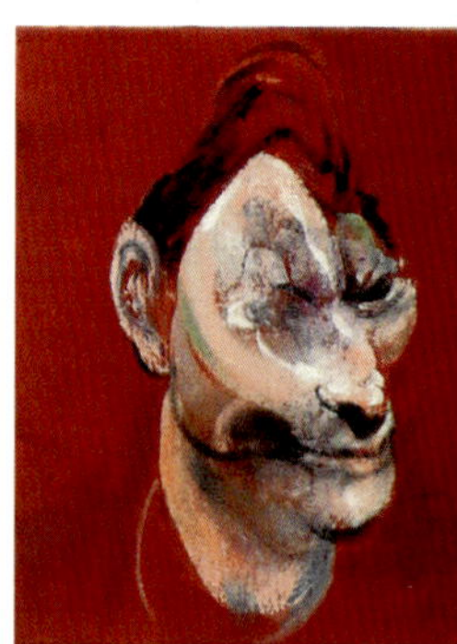

Figure 2: Francis Bacon, *Three Studies for Portrait of Lucian Freud* (1964), © The Estate of Francis Bacon. All rights reserved. DACS 2024. Image, Anthony Devlin, Alamy.

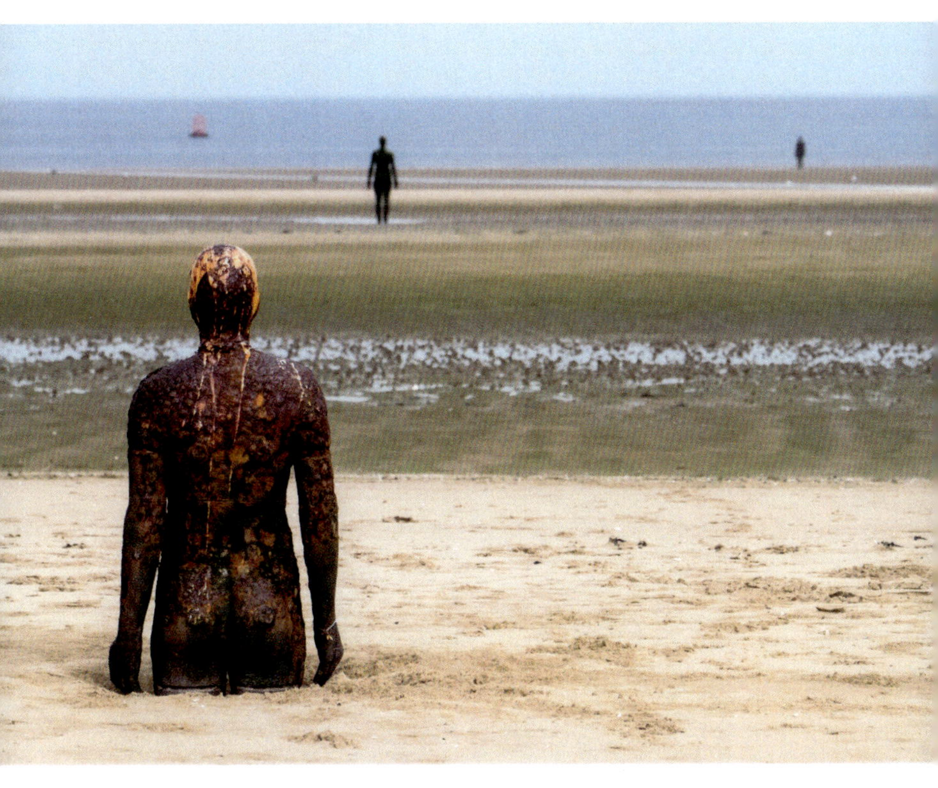

Figure 3: Antony Gormley, *Another Place* (1997).
Image, David Reed, Alamy.

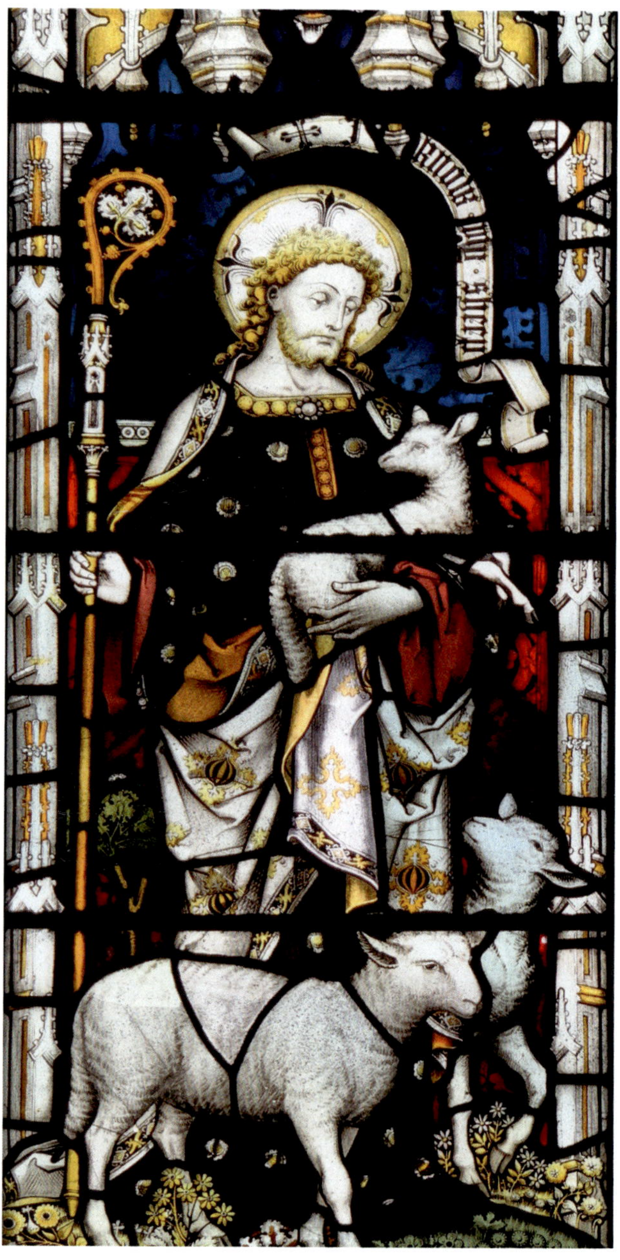

Figure 4: Stained glass, *The Good Shepherd* (1870), Bath Abbey, Bath. Image, Revd Stephen Girling.

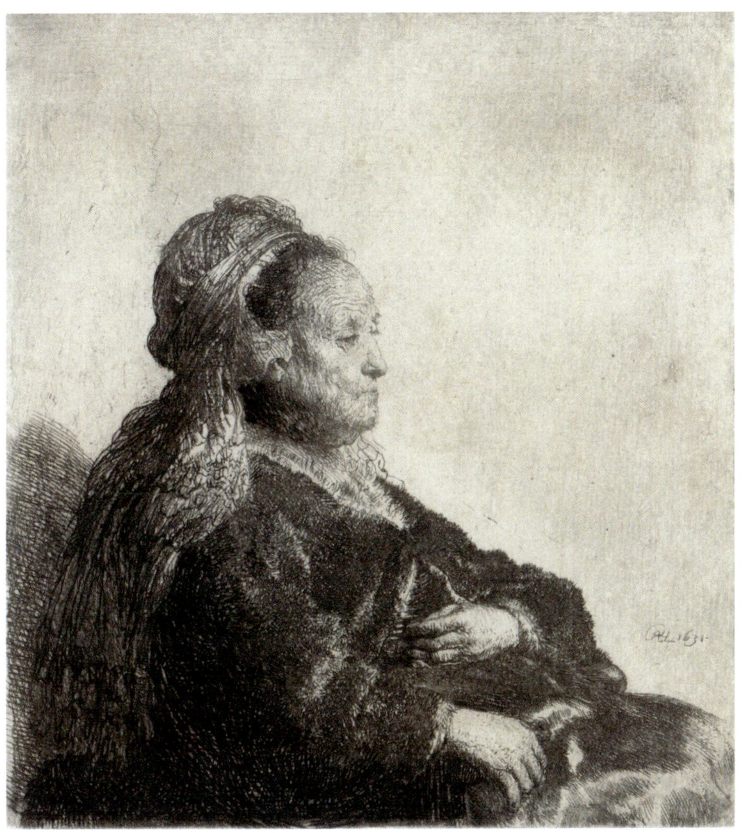

Figure 5: Rembrandt van Rijn, *The Artist's Mother Seated, in an Oriental Headdress, Half Length* (1631), Rijksmuseum, Amsterdam. Image, The Picture Art Collection, Alamy.

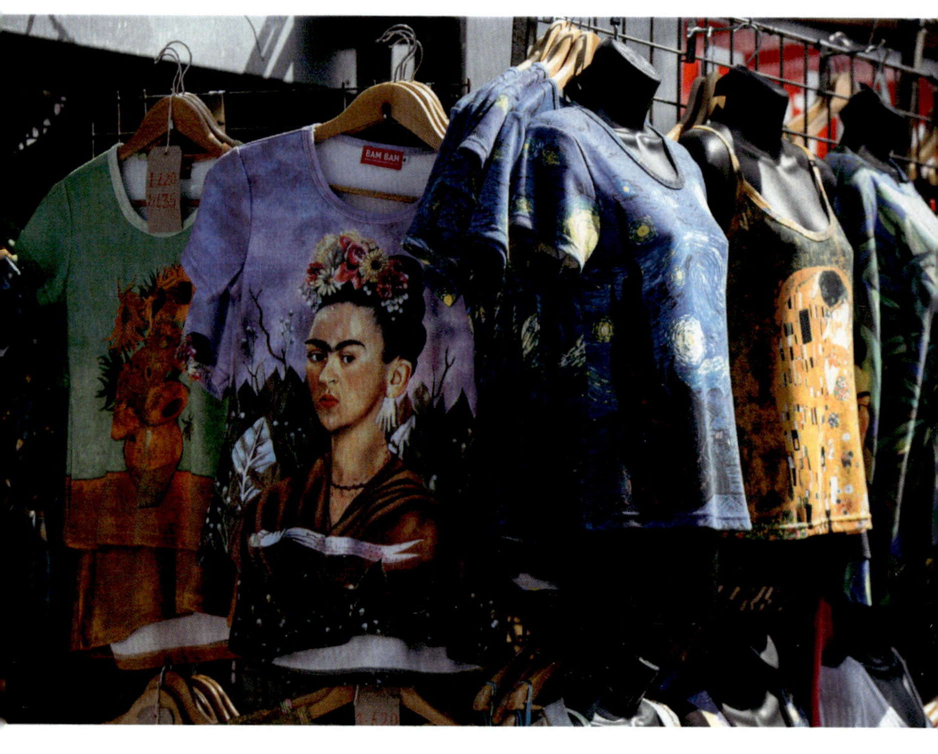

Figure 6: Bettina Strenske, *Quirky fashion on sale at Camden Market* (2016), Alamy.

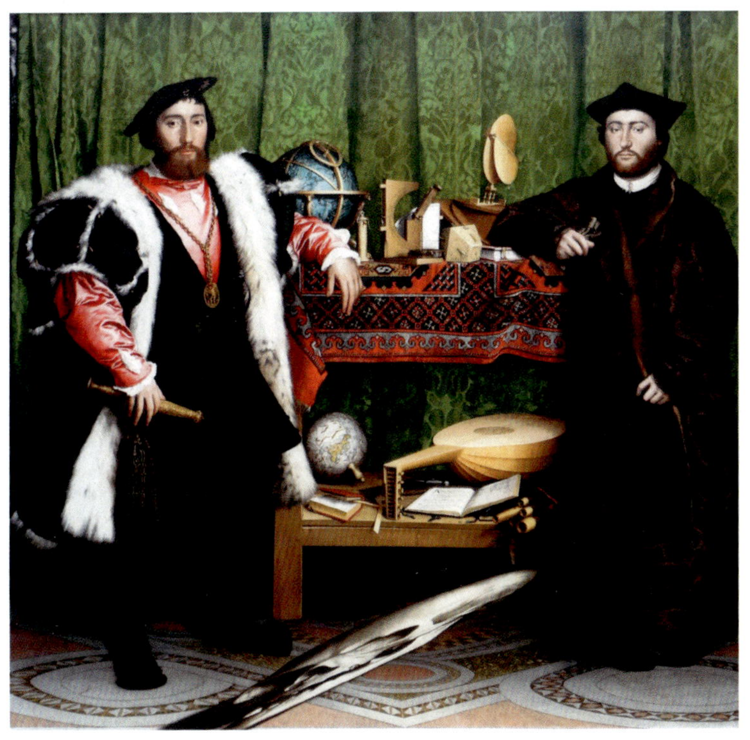

Figure 7: Hans Holbein the Younger,
The Ambassadors (1533), National Gallery, London. Image,
World History Archive, Alamy.

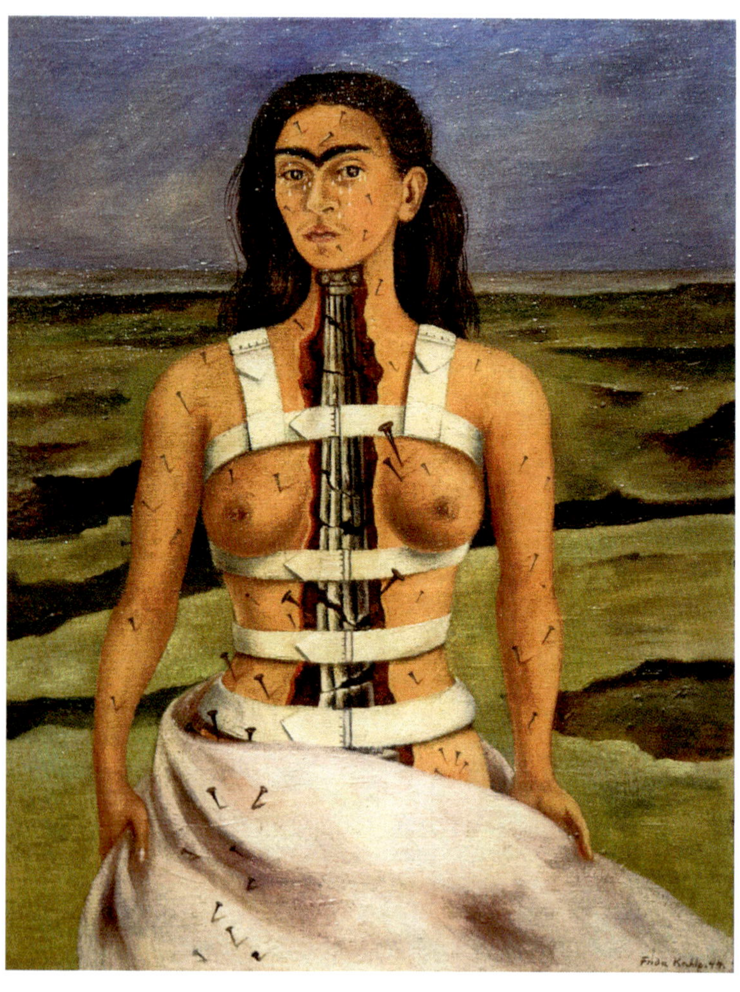

Figure 8: Frida Kahlo, *Broken Column* (1944), Museo Dolores Olmedo, Mexico City. Image, ZUMA Press, Alamy.

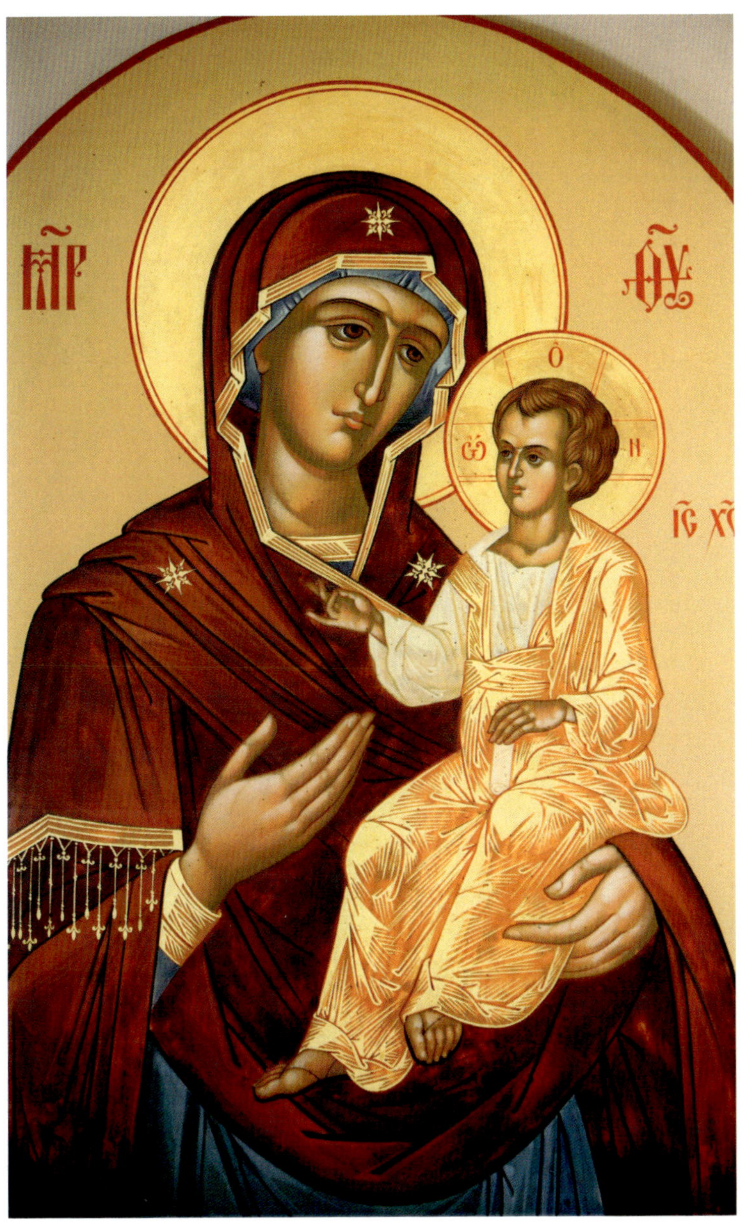

Figure 9: Artist and date unknown, *Icon of Mary and Jesus*, Mary Magdalene Church, Mount of Olives, Jerusalem. Image, Godong, Alamy.

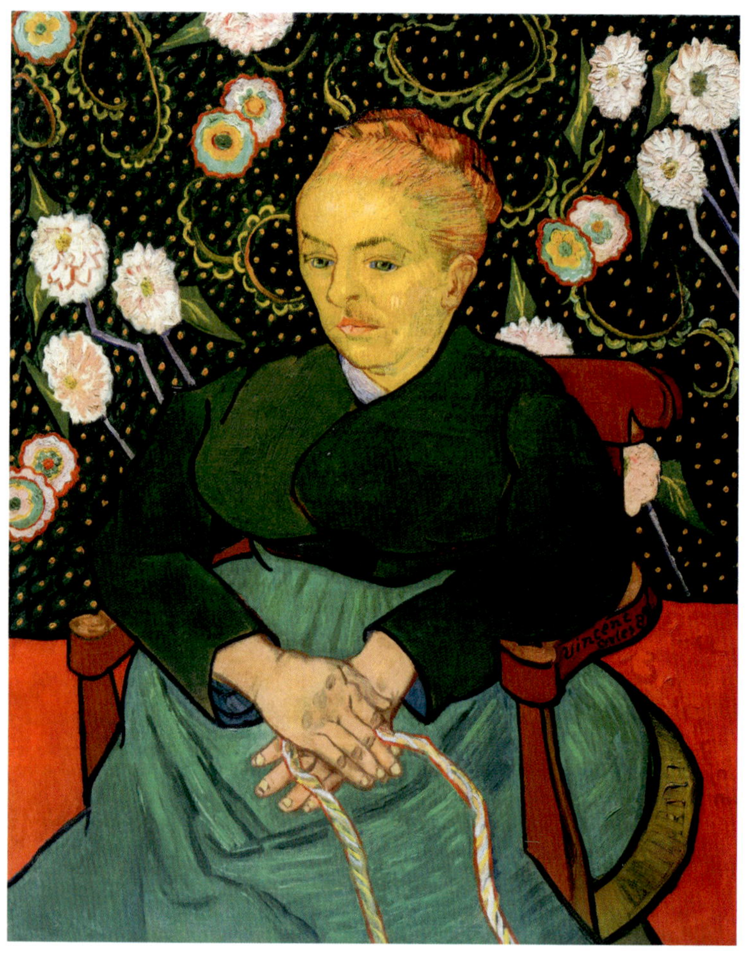

Figure 10: Vincent van Gogh, *La Berceuse* (1889), The Metropolitan Museum of Modern Art.
Image: Incamerastock, Alamy.

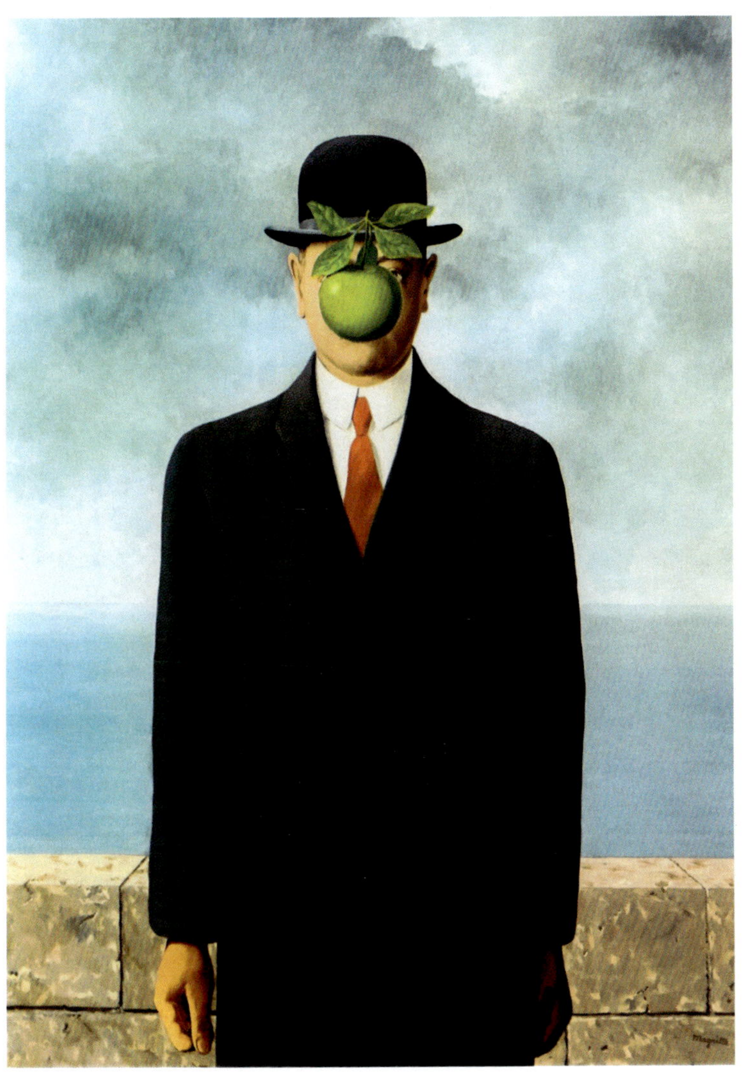

Figure 11: René Magritte, *Son of Man* (1963), Private collection. Image, ROBERT, Alamy.

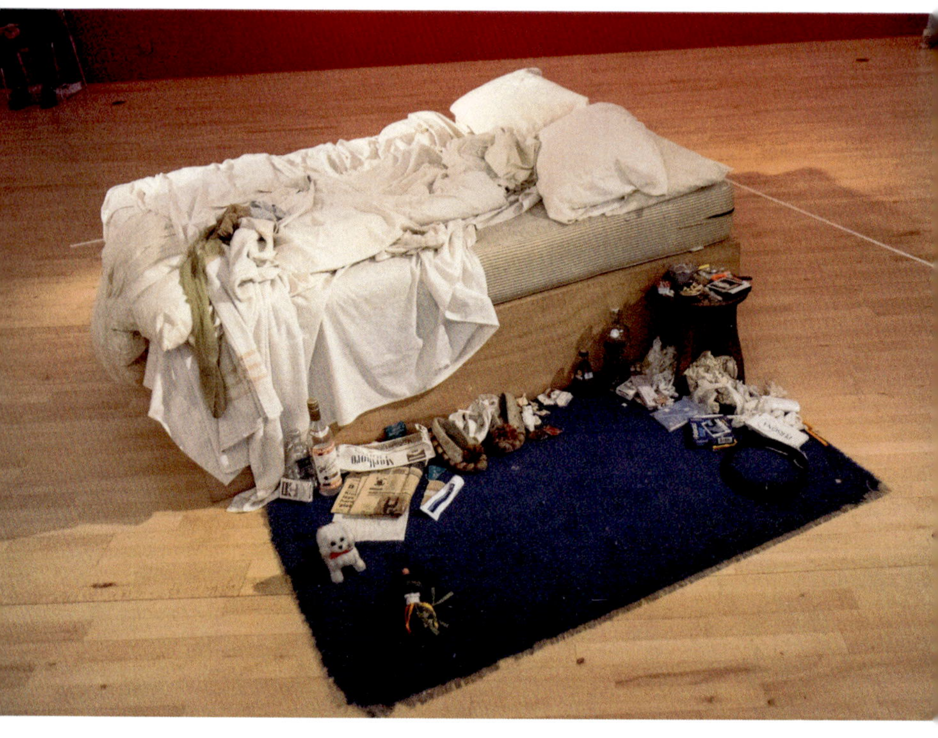

Figure 12: Tracey Emin, *My Bed* (1998), Tate Museum, London. Image, Paul Quayle, Alamy.

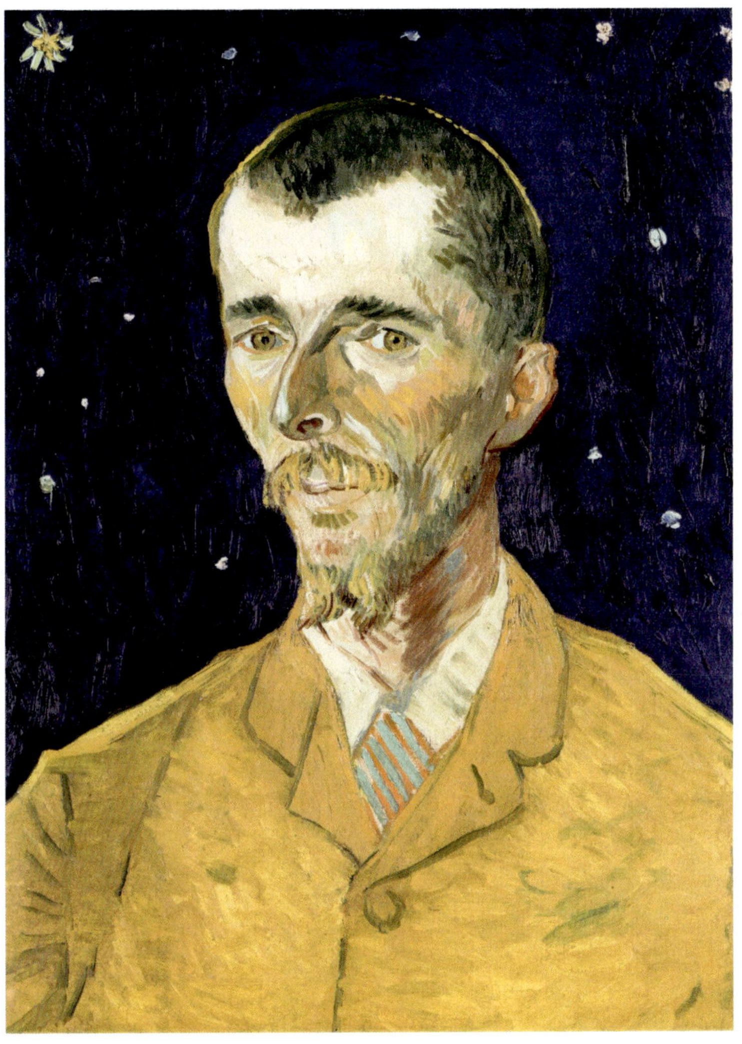

Figure 13: Vincent van Gogh, *Eugene Boch* (1888), Musée D'Orsay, Paris. Image, Incamerastock, Alamy.

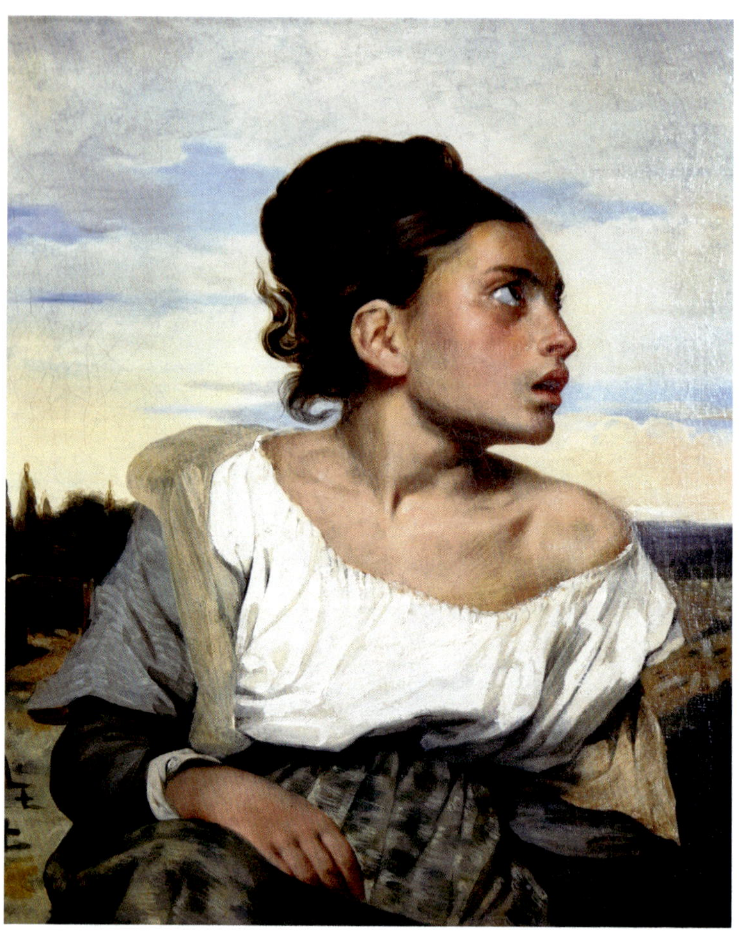

Figure 14: Eugene Delacroix, *Young Orphan Girl in the Cemetery* (1824), Musée du Louvre, Paris. Image, Artelan, Alamy.

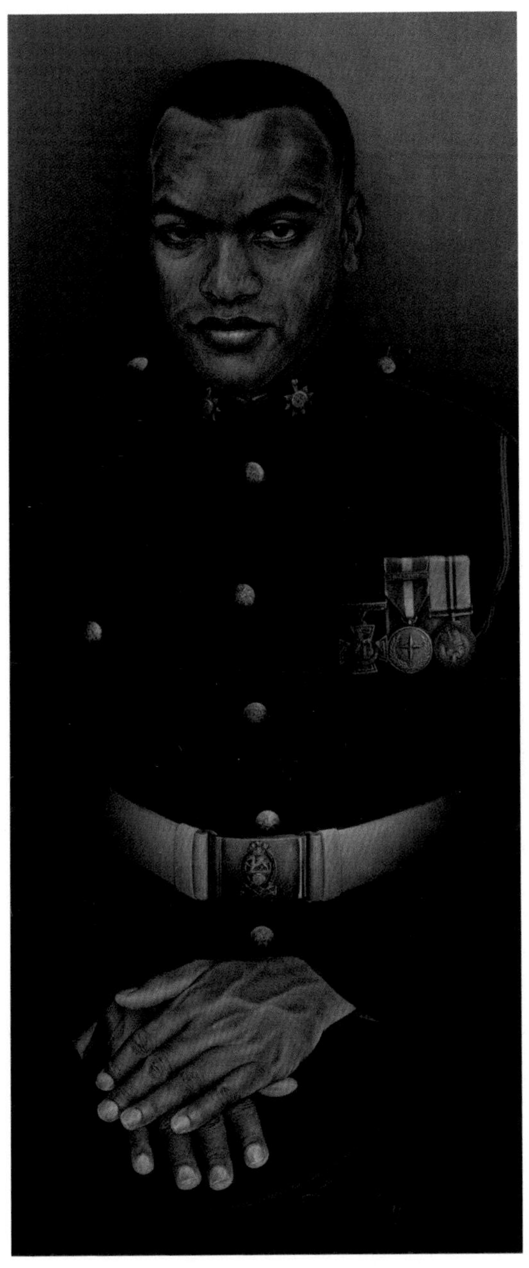

Figure 15: Emma Wesley, *Johnson Gideon Beharry VC* (2006), The National Portrait Gallery, London.

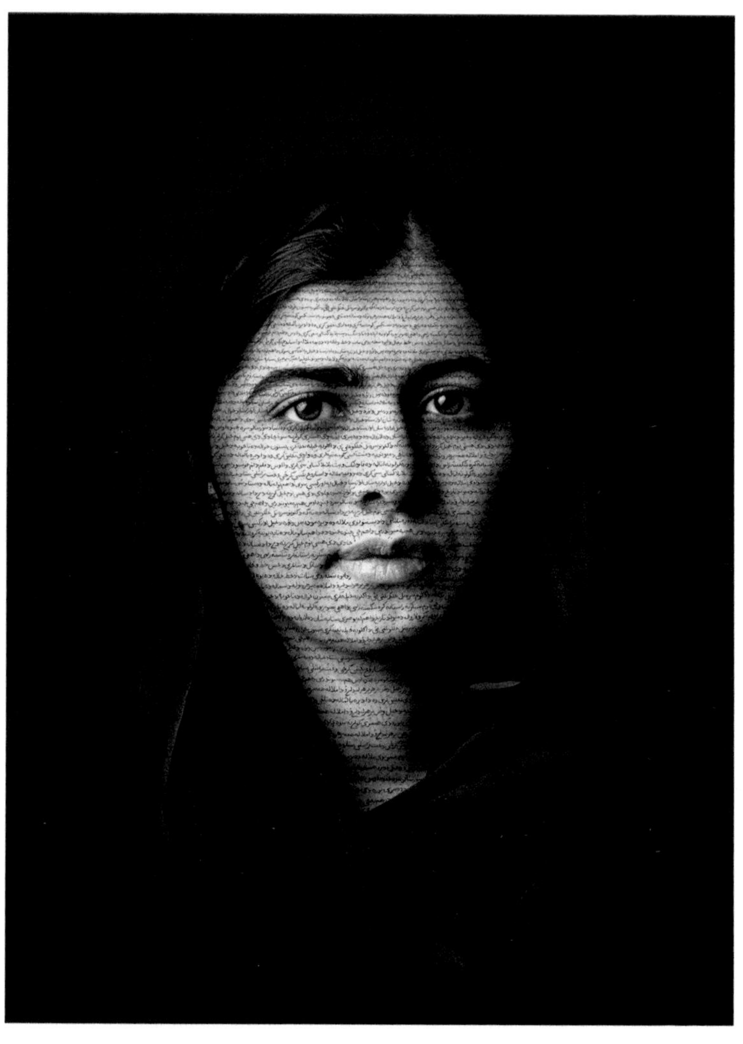

Figure 16: Shirin Neshat, *Malala Yousafzai* (2018),
The National Portrait Gallery, London.

All images used with the permission of the copyright holders.

CHAPTER 4

APPROACHING A PORTRAIT WITH PURPOSE

Idly flicking through a book of art or drifting around a gallery, many of us are inclined to pause at portraits we recognise or like. There are ebbs and flows in our subconscious (born of culture, heritage, and personality), that incline us this way or that. Many of us are disposed towards portraits of people like us, or who look attractive or who break a mould we secretly dislike. Many of us are easily led, lazily guided by democratic or professional opinion, dwelling on portraits deemed worthy of greater respect; Leonardo da Vinci's *Mona Lisa* or Raphael's *Madonna and Child* for example. To see *beyond the face* in a portrait it is essential to learn to navigate these ebbs and flows and be ready to deviate into new directions. We must be willing to make the effort to give deserved attention to others, to value the beautiful diversity within the human race and the importance of making connections with those not like us who are nevertheless also made in the image of God.

First, we must be disciplined to *notice* what is in the portrait, not simply what we see at first glance, but taking the trouble to notice what choices the artist has made. We need to be self-aware, able to notice ourselves as the observer, to register our responses. Acknowledging there is a story behind every subject and every portrait, and that our own story intersects in some way with these, the next step is to register how we *respond* to what we discover about the portrait. Finally, we *reflect* on what is disclosed to us in what we've noticed and responded to and what this might mean for our journey of self-discovery and our understanding of relations with others. To *notice, respond* and *reflect* are the three steps of the method in Chapter 5.

Essential to successful navigation of these three steps are the tools of mindfulness, meditation, and contemplation. With discipline and effort these will help us navigate the ebbs and flows in our subconscious, to truly notice and relate to the person in the portrait, to go *beyond the face* as one person encountering another. These practices are not easily followed because we tend to be self-centred and excitable; it takes determination to be still for long enough and notice what really matters. However, if we make the effort, mindfulness will help us become alive to what *is* and be present to ourselves and the other person, meditation will help us think about what is disclosed to us in the moment and contemplation will take us beyond all the rules and categories of seeing and thinking to a place where our soul is enlarged by the discovery of a truer self in relation to another soul.

MINDFULNESS

Mindfulness is noticing, for example, another's smile, the smell of their perfume, or the way they walk, and accepting these with gratitude. It is giving attention to the present moment, slowing our actions and thoughts to become alive to what *is* and accepting it without judgement. Mindfulness takes us to the still point of a frantic world to discover the freedom of being present in and to the moment. Professor Mark Williams, Emeritus Professor of Clinical Psychology at the University of Oxford, co-developed Mindfulness Based Cognitive Therapy and writes:

> *... mindfulness is to approach our minds and bodies with a sense of curiosity, openness, and acceptance so that we may see what is here to be discovered and be with it without so much struggling. In this way, little by little, we begin to release ourselves from the grip of our old habits of mind. (21)*

Mindfulness pauses our analytical and imaginative thought processes, these may be indispensable for problem-solving, but they tend to take our mind far away from the present moment, from actual sensory experience and true encounter. It helps us notice sensory stimuli for what they are (and the thoughts and feelings induced), to register and validate them without judgement. Mindfulness accords equal worth to body and soul, so that what is sensed in our body and intuited in our soul is given permission to register itself in the conversation of our mind.

When we casually look at another person, we scarcely have time to notice them before our mind spins off into thought and judgement and our imagination into novel conjectures. We might look at someone and find ourselves thinking that they are overweight or unhappy or find ourselves taking an instant dislike. In a sense these are mental events on a par with noticing that they are carrying a red handbag or wearing brogues. However, 'overweight', 'unhappy' and 'beautiful' are pejorative judgements and not neutral observations, we see them according to 'our image' of how they are or might otherwise be, not how they actually are; and we are the poorer for it. Over time, repeatedly unchecked and unquestioned thoughts etch deeper and deeper creases into our minds and become fertile ground for prejudice and discrimination. Mindfulness recognises casual observation for what it is and establishes an intent to be enriched by a true encounter with another.

Giving attention to our body is a good way to establish mindful habits, to notice in our breathing the air passing through our nostrils and the rise and fall of our diaphragm, to rest in the gift of each breath. We can also notice the touch of the clothes upon our skin, the weight of our feet upon the ground, the complex sensations in our eyes and ears. When being mindful we easily become distracted so it's helpful to have an 'anchor point' to recentre and retune us to our original intention. This might be a disciplined return to the rhythm of our breathing, to the sight of a flickering candle or to a quiet repetition of a simple word or phrase. In the Christian tradition the prayers 'Come Lord Jesus' or 'Lord Have Mercy' are repeated vocally or silently to return the wandering mind to the present.

Living in the moment is an art that is best learned in daily life, intentionally noticing what *is*, with acceptance and gratitude. Brushing our teeth, commuting to work, eating out – the more frequently we become aware of ourselves, others and our surroundings, the easier it will be to mindfully notice when choosing to look at the another's face in a portrait.

Mindful attention to our senses and the way our body is responding to another person is an important step in going *beyond the face* and forms the basis of *noticing* in the three-step method. Giving careful attention to thoughts and intuitions is difficult for those of us living in cultures obsessed with instant results, fine image, success and prowess. Ultimately it's through the next steps of meditation and contemplation that we will be able to navigate the defensive self-interest that mitigates against sustained attention, to surrender of our whole person to God and the image of God in the other. In so doing our true self will be disclosed.

MEDITATION

Meditation helps us ponder on that which has been disclosed to us through our senses, by way of an inner conversation. It harnesses the faculties of the mind, imagination and fantasy and helps us evaluate and relate to ourselves, to others and to the natural world. Meditation hosts a thoughtful space in which we attempt to stand outside of ourselves and our small-minded ways, to give us a while in which to negotiate with 'propaganda' and to form appropriate responses. Professor Mark Williams writes about meditation giving us:

> *a vantage point from which we can witness our own thoughts and feelings as they arise. It takes us off the hair-trigger that compels us to react to things as soon as they happen. (22)*

Western cultures treat meditation as a private discipline, a tool for the inner journey of self-discovery and self-improvement. This narrow 'i-world' contrasts with the more social world of Eastern cultures in which human well-being is intimately bound up with relations to others, to 'God' and the earth. This relational paradigm is essential if we are to use meditation to go *beyond the face* of another in a portrait. Returning to the South African principle of Ubuntu, that 'a person is only a person through other people,' if mindfulness helps us acknowledge what our senses present to us in the presence of the other, meditation helps our minds stand down from first reactions, from creating new realities born of our deepest fears and desires, and helps us to get to 'know' the other in order to become more of who we are, as we immerse ourselves in their story.

This is more difficult than it sounds, many of us have highly defensive or opinionated thoughts in the presence of a stranger. Fearing for our safety our mind tends to act like that of a new parent protecting their baby: we are often suspicious and at the mercy of our vulnerabilities. From a lifetime of warnings about 'stranger danger,' unchallenged prejudice, insecurity, and apathy towards others unlike us, we have remained cocooned in our own small minds, keeping the other at a safe distance. For meditation to be profitable we must be willing to be vulnerable to the stranger, to surrender to the removing of our 'masks' and the dismantling of our social defences. We must be willing to make the effort to rediscover the humanity lost to us since we grew out of childhood, to be reconciled to ourselves, the other and to God. We must have the courage to leave the comfort of our familiar world. Jesus said;

If any want to become my followers, let them deny themselves and take up their cross daily and follow me. For those who want to save their life will lose it, and those who lose their life for my sake will save it. What does it profit them if they gain the whole world, but lose or forfeit themselves? Luke 9:23-25

Most religious traditions use meditation to help their adherents 'deny themselves' by honouring a higher being more significant than they. In the Christian tradition Lectio Divina (divine reading) and Visio Divina (divine seeing) involve the repeated reading of a biblical text or image. Whereas traditional study methods involve the student examining a text or image for meaning, Lectio and Visio Divina are forms of meditation whereby they prayerfully submit themselves to examination by God through the medium of the text or image.

Like mindfulness, meditation is best learned in everyday life. We can be more intentional about how we get to know a stranger, giving them the time they deserve and letting down our own 'masks' of invulnerability. As we consume the daily news, we can think about how our minds are processing what we hear and where our imaginations take us, and rather than hop from one social media post to the next in a constant pursuit of stimulation we can press pause and take a moment to ponder what our minds are up to and why. Reviewing thoughts, feelings, actions, and motivations, in moments of quiet reflection, will protect us from the unhealthy undercurrents of our inner world, the outer forces of trend and the narratives of our self-interested 'tribes'.

Meditation is the basis of the final two steps in the three-step method, affording us the opportunity to pause our grasshopper minds and discover what is being disclosed to us in the face of another as we give time for their story to intersect with, confront and reshape ours.

CONTEMPLATION

Mindfulness and meditation use our everyday faculties of sense and thought to take us beyond another's face, to know ourselves better as a relational person. We become better able to live well, to be reconciled to ourselves in all that we are, and be reconcilers in a world which carries so much suspicion, prejudice, and ignorance.

To cement these gains and go even further we can use our imaginations to go beyond the immediacy of another's face and beyond physical senses and thinking altogether, to a holy ground; a place where two human souls encounter each other in the presence of God, because of whom both are spiritual beings.

Contemplation is a practice for finding this ground and for 'abiding' there and is essential if we wish to transcend the limits of our everyday sensing and thinking.

We are touching this holy ground when we fall in love, or experience the miracle of birth, or find ourselves relating to another person in a unique way because of a mutual 'chemistry'. Some discover it as they journey with a loved one through terminal illness when all endeavours to cure or explain have ceased. Some are touching it in the new and 'invisible' ways they find to relate to a family member who has been robbed of speech, memory, and cognition by Alzheimer's disease. In all these instances we are drawing upon instincts of a relational self beyond the everyday senses and all capacities of thought, understanding and feeling. For those with spiritual faith this is a manifestation of the infinite love of God making itself present, reminding us of what we once took for granted in the wide-eyed innocence of childhood trust and wonder in relation to both other people and the world about us. We are sensing the reality that that which is finite in our sensory world is only an echo of the infinite, in which all things find their consummation. The Trappist monk and contemplative teacher Thomas Merton wrote:

For the world and time are the dance of the Lord in emptiness. The silence of the spheres is the music of a wedding feast. The more we persist in misunderstanding the phenomena of life, the more we analyze them out into strange finalities and complex purposes of our own, the more we involve ourselves in sadness, absurdity and despair. But it does not matter much, because no despair of ours can alter the reality of things; or stain the joy of the cosmic dance which is always there. (23)

In that which lies beyond our everyday senses and capacities of thought we are being called upon to be open to recognising the true reality of things which Merton describes as the cosmic dance, on this 'holy ground' where our soul and the soul of the other are one in God.

While mindfulness and meditation nurture good habits of noticing, responding and reflecting essential to the three-step method, contemplation stills us to that which is beyond sense and thinking, to a wordless resting in the presence of God in whom we are alive, a presence beyond words, thoughts and images. If mindfulness and meditation are active disciplines of intention, contemplation is a passive submission of body and soul to that which is their infinite source and sustenance and by which we have any agency at all. Contemplation conceives all that we are as 'gift' (including the other person in a portrait), and in submission to God as the giver it seeks for no further reward save that of knowing we are all loved.

Contemplation of the face in a portrait harnesses stillness and silence to 'undo' familiarity and open us out into a liminal place, onto a threshold of discovery in which we become momentarily attuned to that which **is,** the very ground of our being. It is that moment in which to know is to know that we are both known, to love is to know that we are both first loved: and love bows down towards the image of the divine in the other person. That which previously divided us yields, it is dissolved away.

Anything near complete submission to the other person or to God is extremely difficult. Those who take this path will spend a lifetime learning how to let go of the habits of the ego and of sensory desire, to live as those who are simply loved. The sixteenth-century priest St John of the Cross found his way through what he called the 'dark night of the soul', a purging of desire in contempt for the lie that anything less than the infinite love of God will satisfy. To gather what we need for such a journey into the infinite love that completely embraces both us and the other person in a portrait, means persistently assuming a wilful disposition of surrender to this love. We will discover in the very first inklings of our heart being 'recalibrated' by the love of God, a holy ground – and in joyful humility we will be drawn onward, rediscovering more and more of who we and the other truly are.

Contemplation is less of a discipline and more a disposition of the soul. It is best cultivated through intentional, regular removal into stillness and silence, to a place where sensory stimulation is minimal. Rituals which help include the repetition of mantras (see 'meditation' above) with a gradual shift away from words towards silence and a pared down awareness of our breathing, allowing ourselves to be beheld by a religious Icon or listening to the decaying notes of a singing bowl. All these incline us towards the still centre of the body, the ground of our being.

Contemplation is seasoned through intentions in daily life. Some recalibrate their looking in nature, to a finer and finer scale, to a contemplative gaze beyond the measure of things. Thomas Merton paid close attention to the sacramental presence of nature, its pointing beyond itself to that of which it is only an echo:

> *When we are alone on a starlit night, when by chance we see the migrating birds in autumn descending on a grove of junipers to rest and eat; when we see children in*

a moment when they are really children, when we know love in our own hearts; or when, like the Japanese poet, Basho, we hear an old frog land in a quiet pond with a solitary splash – at such times the awakening, the turning inside out of all values, the 'newness,' the emptiness and the purity of vision that make themselves evident, all these provide a glimpse of the cosmic dance. (24)

Poetry can also help establish this contemplative posture, for in poetry language and form dispose words to surrender a meaning which is beyond themselves. Poetry discloses new worlds within the known world, that we might be more 'at home' with ourselves, the other or the natural world.

For some the contemplative disposition becomes a nurtured response to increasing physical or mental frailty. The Jesuit priest, Pedro Arrupe, spent the last ten years of his life living with the after-effects of a stroke:

More than ever, I find myself in the hands of God. This is what I have wanted all my life from my youth. But now there is a difference; the initiative is entirely with God. It is indeed a profound spiritual experience to know and feel myself so totally in God's hands. (25)

Etty Hillesum was a Dutch Jew who had a religious awakening while living under the horrors of Nazi occupation in Amsterdam. Before she was deported to Auschwitz where she was killed, she journeyed through a long period of contemplative surrender, being gifted an extraordinary sense of the unity of all things normally divided, including Jewish collaborators, her German captors and even the land on which they lived:

> *The bare trunks that climb past my window now shelter under a cover of young green leaves. A springy fleece along their naked, tough, ascetic limbs. I went to bed early last night, and from my bed I stared out through the large open window. And it was once more as if life with all its mysteries was close to me, as if I could touch it. I had the feeling that I was resting against the naked breast of life and could feel her gentle and regular heartbeat. I felt safe and protected. And I thought, how strange. It is wartime. There are concentration camps. (26)*

To contemplate that which lies beyond our face and the face in a portrait takes intentional effort and surrender and involves personal vulnerability. This effort is richly rewarded in the rediscovery our truer self. It is not the easy reward of knowledge but the hard-won reward of knowing something of that which is beyond our senses and beyond thought – something that arises in the encounter between two persons with souls.

CONCLUSION

As many of us tire of the fast pace of life and the constant pressures to possess more and to be 'out there' in the marketplace of opinion, the rediscovery of the ancient practices of mindfulness, meditation and contemplation are giving us the tools with which we can resist and find a truer way to be and to relate to others. As the world gets smaller and proximity to others increases in both the digital and physical realms, these tools can help us overcome the forces that incline us to ignore or dismiss the other person, which diminishes everyone and in the extreme, left unchecked, leads to suspicion, discrimination and conflict. These tools are essential to the three-step method in the following chapter and like anything worthwhile, to most of us they won't come naturally. To learn how to use them will take effort and will mean paying close attention to ourselves and others, an effort that will be immensely rewarding and that our fractured and rapidly changing world needs us to make.

CHAPTER 5

THE THREE-STEP METHOD

In the three-step method to go *beyond the face*, '*Noticing*' uses techniques in mindfulness to help us see what is there and what is going on in ourselves as we look. '*Responding*' uses learning and meditation to disclose how we see ourselves and the subject. '*Reflecting*' in meditation and contemplation helps us discern new and better ways of relating both to ourselves and to the subject.

What follows are guidelines and tips for each step and will become more natural if used in conjunction with the everyday practices of mindfulness, meditation and contemplation suggested in Chapter 4. While far from exhaustive, they will help establish good habits of looking and seeing, both at ourselves and another person. Chapter 6 provides examples with which to practise the method.

STEP 1: LOOKING – TO NOTICE

Resisting all impulses to evaluate or analyse what you see in the portrait, in Step 1 simply register what you notice in both a general sense and in the fine detail.

- What is the posture of the subject? Are they posed for the artist or captured in the state of some action or activity?

- How much of the subject can you see, are they full length, half-length, head and shoulders or is only their face shown?

- What's their expression, both in their face and in the body language of their pose?

- What's the look in their eyes and do you notice other features in their face or on their body?

- What do you notice about the colour of their skin, or their hair or other bodily features?

- Where is the light coming from? It might be from multiple directions.

- Roughly what age are they?

- How are they dressed, are they wearing jewellery, do they have tattoos or another form of body adornment?

- Are there objects placed on or with the subject or elsewhere in the image?

- Are there any symbols, including words or letters?

- What is the background and setting of the portrait? How is the subject placed within it?

- Look at scale, are there aspects of the subject or background which are given greater or lesser prominence?

- What medium has the artist chosen for the image and what is the surface texture?

- How has the portrait been framed?

- What stylistic choices has the artist made? Is the image realistic, figurative, abstract, expressionist or symbolic in its manner of representation?

- Does the portrait have a title and is it signed by the artist?

- What else do you notice?

It may be helpful to make a record of what you've noticed.

Next, go on to ask what you notice about yourself as the one who is looking. Again, **avoid all analysis and evaluation** and simply notice yourself. For example:

- Do you have a visceral (gut) reaction?

- What are your feelings? Do you feel comfortable?

- What do you like or dislike?

- What are you attracted to or repelled by?

- Is your eye drawn to one aspect of the portrait more than another?

- Are you struggling to notice and not to analyse?

STEP 2: LOOKING – TO RESPOND

Before looking again at the face in the portrait to respond to it, learn what you can about the subject, the artist and the nature of any commission. Chapter 3 gives more detail about the type of information which will be helpful. Much will depend on the provenance of the portrait, but you might learn about:

- The past and present life of the subject, both prior to and at the time of the making of their portrait.

- The artist, their worldview, values and beliefs.

- Any pre-existing relationship between the artist and the subject.

- The nature of the commission, any relationship of the artist or subject to the patron and whether the intent was to display the portrait in a particular context.

- The subject or theme of the portrait from a summary description provided by the curator.

- The genre or style of portraiture used by the artist, its particular strengths and weaknesses.

- Any objects, dress or adornment used in the portrait.

- The context and any significance of the backdrop or scene, or other (secondary) subjects.

- Any cultural, religious, or social references.

- Other portraits of the same subject or by the same artist which provide contrast and shed light on the choices made in this instance.

With what you have learned you now know the subject better. The aim now is to look again at the portrait in order to respond to the subject – as two human beings with a common humanity, with life stories having points of connection and divergence, of resonance and dissonance. In 'looking to respond' imagine yourself being looked at or spoken to by the subject of the portrait and notice your responses. It's essential that you give time to this step and continue **to avoid evaluation and analysis**. The responses you notice might include:

- Connections between their life story and yours.

- Sympathy or aversion towards the subject and/or others like them.

- Prejudices connected with indications of race or gender or religion.

- Differences of belief or worldview that intrigue or create a distance between you.

- Memories of a past experience or of another person.

- Feelings of attraction, guilt, anger, or displeasure.

- A visceral reaction such as a gut feeling or a change of body temperature or heartrate.

- A judgemental attitude for or against some aspect of the subject or their life.

It's important that in noticing your responses to the subject you remain neutral towards them and simply register them without evaluation or judgement. It may be helpful to record your responses. In Step 3 you will use these responses to help you be more fully alive to yourself, to the other and to God.

STEP 3: LOOKING – TO REFLECT

In this step you will use techniques of meditation and contemplation to harness powers of thought, imagination and intuition.

Look again at the portrait and allow yourself time to analyse and evaluate what you have noticed about yourself and your responses. The aim is to gain a better understanding of yourself, your strengths and weaknesses, and if and how you want to change. Meditate upon your responses (turn them over in your mind), you might for example reflect on why or how:

- this (and not that) 'struck' you? Why now?

- You made assumptions which were not supported by the facts you found out in Step 2. You might see how you have been indifferent to the truth and followed 'groupthink'.

- You noticed prejudice or partiality.

- You had a particular visceral or emotional reaction.

- You were ignorant of what you should have known.

- You were influenced by your heritage, experience, culture, personality, likes, or dislikes.

- You were surprised, pleased, disappointed, or confused by the feelings, thoughts or insights you noticed.

- You have failed to be generous or compassionate towards certain people or groups.

- The subject of the portrait has been a gift to you.

It may be helpful to note down what arises from your reflections.

If you wish to, go beyond meditation into contemplation: beyond reflecting on what you received through your physical senses and thoughts, into the realm of intuition. This is related to your senses and thoughts but is not limited to them or constrained by them. All these faculties of body and soul are part of our common humanity as human beings and so in openness to one another (and to God), trust that a better way of being and of relating will be disclosed. If you find contemplation difficult or confusing, re-read the section on contemplation in Chapter 4 and try some of the daily practices. This will help cultivate this particular disposition for going *beyond the face*.

CONCLUSION

The description 'three-step method' makes it sound simple, however we soon discover (especially those of us who have been educated in the Western world), that it is difficult to notice without evaluation and analysis, to slow down sufficiently to truly see that which we've remained blind to for a long while, whether by choice or ignorance. For those of us who persist, who stay the course because we know it's only in relation to others that we become truly who we are, we will discover riches. Moreover, a world which is repeatedly fractured by suspicion, prejudice and intolerance, by 'othering the other', desperately needs people who bother to take the trouble to cultivate empathy with those who are different and to whom they've taken a dislike.

In anticipating the three-step method we may have an awareness of a prejudice or partiality towards another and be approaching a portrait with the goal of changing how we think or feel. It's likely however, that we'll get caught up in the process of the method: remembering the guidance, hoping to discover something significant, not wanting to waste our time. Indeed, our goals and the method itself might limit our discovery, our appreciation of that which is being disclosed to us. This is when further time spent in meditation and / or contemplation may be richly rewarding as we continue to make the effort to lay aside all goals and expectations, ours and others', to rest with what is disclosed and, remaining in the moment, to trust the outcome to look after itself. Bearing in mind we are inclined to see and believe what we want (as opposed to what we ought or need), it will invariably be helpful to talk our reflections through with another person who knows us well. Finally, only with the benefit of hindsight and in the longer term will we be able to see the rewards of having taken the time to look *beyond the face.*

CHAPTER 6
PRACTICE AND METHOD

C hapter 1 chronicled the extraordinary growth in the availability of portraits, once the preserve of churches and galleries but now freely available in the physical and digital worlds. None of us has to go very far to find a portrait with which to practise the three-step method. Scrolling through our digital gallery or gazing at a face on a billboard as we wait for a tube train, in a few moments we can swing into action and apply ourselves to seeing *beyond the face*. However, until we're more experienced, we are likely to find we've mastered the method but have not reaped the rewards. For this we need to make the disciplined effort of drawing on the wisdom of others who have gone before us, and committing to practice and experiment.

PRACTICE

Firstly, find a portrait in a form that will be easy for you to spend time with and one for which you have access to information, at least about the subject but ideally also about the artist and the commission. To practise, choose a time when you will be undisturbed and be able to concentrate without distraction, having with you a means of making notes.

Cultivating a new way of looking takes time, so be kind to yourself and don't expect too much too soon. Repeatedly returning to the same portrait will build confidence, especially if you are able to learn new things about the portrait when you return to it after first looking, and if are able to give time to meditation and/or contemplation when you are not directly looking at it.

There is merit in working with portraits whose subjects are strangers (whether dead or alive), because far removed from any prior relationship you will be able to take a more objective viewpoint. This will bring clarity to the three-step method and you'll be more easily surprised by what is disclosed, and so be encouraged to keep on practising.

Each of the following four examples comprises an image and collated information for the initial stage of Step 2. It is essential NOT to read the collated information before Step 1 is complete.

1. Eugene Boch, Vincent van Gogh **(Figure 13)**

Where an artist has left (accessible) information about a portrait and the thought processes behind it, this is invaluable for Step 2. This portrait by Van Gogh is unusual in two respects. Firstly Van Gogh's letters give far-reaching insights into the subject of the portrait and into the artist's thoughts and state of mind at the time he painted it, and secondly the subject is a portrait 'type' (poet).

This portrait of Belgian artist Eugene Boch was painted by Van Gogh when he lived in Arles in the South of France. At the time Van Gogh was getting very impatient with Paul Gaugin, the artist whose long-delayed arrival in Arles was frustrating their plans to form a community or association of artists. Over the preceding months Van Gogh had vacillated between hope and despair but he was sustained by sincere admiration for Gaugin who he referred to as a great artist and a new poet for their time. Van Gogh had invested a great deal of thought, energy, and money in a home for this community at the Yellow House where he was living.

This vision absorbed the energy and passion that a few years earlier Van Gogh had channelled into serving the poor. In his early twenties he was an evangelical Christian with a missionary zeal. He trained as an evangelist, living and working for two years among poor miners and peasants in a district of Belgium called the Borinage. He gave his all, sacrificing all personal comfort to serve them (following the example of Christ). However his speaking abilities were considered too poor for this training to continue. Around the same time Van Gogh fell out with his father and grandfather, both ministers in the Dutch Reformed Church, over a love-interest of Van Gogh's they disagreed with. Van Gogh finally turned his back on formal religion and over the years his spirituality took on the character of Christian humanism, animated by insights of mysticism. This is evident in a letter he wrote to his brother Theo on the day he painted this portrait.

I'd like to paint men or women with that je ne sais quoi of the eternal, of which the halo used to be the symbol, and which we try to achieve through the radiance itself, through the vibrancy of our colorations …… Ah, the portrait – the portrait with the model's thoughts, his soul – it so much seems to me that it must come. (27) 3rd Sept 1888

Van Gogh was aiming to paint a consoling portrait of a

poet, with something of the eternal about it, reaching into the soul. A few weeks before this portrait was painted Van Gogh described what he had in mind:

I'd like to do the portrait of an artist friend who dreams great dreams, who works as the nightingale sings, because that's his nature ... I'm now going to be an arbitrary colourist. I exaggerate the blond of the hair, I come to orange tones, chromes, pale lemon. Behind the head — instead of painting the dull wall of the mean room, I paint the infinite. I make a simple background of the richest, most intense blue that I can prepare, and with this simple combination, the brightly lit blond head, against this rich blue background achieves a mysterious effect, like a star in the deep azure. (28)
18th August 1888

Eugene Boch sat twice to model for Van Gogh who had written that important subjects should not be attempted from memory or imagination but from the pose of a model.

On 3rd October 1888 in a letter to Gaugin, Van Gogh describes Gaugin as a 'new poet' who will awaken a new era as did the renaissance poets in their own time. Of these Van Gogh had especially in mind the fourteenth-century poet Petrarch who he admired, who at times had lived in nearby Avignon. Petrarch was considered the father of humanism and of the renaissance, a devout Catholic who saw the divine as intimately part of the everyday concreteness of life (as opposed to a God 'on high' making occasional supernatural interventions). This was a way of seeing things that was entirely resonant with Van Gogh's own. Gaugin is the 'new Petrarch' and to demonstrate his importance this portrait of Boch was one of two Van Gogh hung above his bed at the Yellow House. A month later he wrote to Gaugin:

> *It won't take you long to discover, under all the modernity, the ancient world and the Renaissance, which is sleeping. Now, as far as they're concerned, you're at liberty to reawaken them. (29)* 3rd October 1888

However, Boch soon became more than a model, he became a close friend to Van Gogh, sharing a common love for Belgium and especially for the region of the Borinage. They even discussed the possibility of Boch setting up a Northern 'outpost' of the Arles community, with artists travelling in-between the two. The day after he sat for the portrait, Boch left Arles to go to the Borinage to paint coalminers and coal mines. Van Gogh later wrote to him:

I sincerely hope that our relationship, once embarked upon, will last for good. Because everything you do will be of extraordinary interest to me, since I so much love that sad region of the Borinage, which will always be unforgettable to me. (30) 2nd October **1888**

This portrait was painted at a time in Van Gogh's life which was fertile with possibility: the awakening of long-lost renaissance ideals, the birth of a community of artists committed to these ideals, the vision and passion of the poet-artist Paul Gaugin, the extension of Vincent's vision to the region of the Borinage and a new friendship for Van Gogh and Eugene Boch. At the portrait's completion Van Gogh writes:

So I'm still between two currents of ideas, the first, material difficulties, turning this way and that to build up an existence, and then the study of colour. I still have hopes of finding something there. To express the love of two lovers through a marriage of two complementary colours, their mixture and their contrasts, the mysterious vibrations of adjacent tones. To express the thought of a forehead through the radiance of a light tone on a dark background. To express hope through some star. The ardour of a living being through the rays of a setting sun. That's certainly not trompe-l'oeil

realism, but isn't it something that really exists? (31)
3rd September 1888

When Gaugin arrived later in October their sixty-three days together were full of the violent extremes of hope and despair born of two unsuited temperaments whose respective visions proved mis-aligned. Meanwhile Van Gogh's mental health had become increasingly fragile and their ambitions for the artists' community at the Yellow House were finally shattered with the now infamous self-mutilation of Van Gogh's ear. Awareness of his fragile mental state even before the arrival of Gaugin is evident in Van Gogh's letter to his sister soon after painting this portrait:

> *My dear sister, I believe that at present we must paint nature's rich and magnificent aspects; we need good cheer and happiness, hope and love. The uglier, older, meaner, iller, poorer I get, the more I wish to take my revenge by doing brilliant colour, well arranged, resplendent. (32)* 14th September 1888

After Van Gogh and his brother Theo died in 1890, Theo's wife gave the portrait to Eugene Boch as a souvenir of the two brothers, a testament to affection. In 1940, when Eugene Boch lay dying at home, his sister

Anna was with him and wrote in her diary of Boch's admiration for his friend Vincent and of this beautiful portrait hanging near his bed.

2. **Young Orphan Girl in the Cemetery**, Eugene Delacroix **(Figure 14)**

Sometimes very little information is available about the subject of a portrait, or they are known to be an imaginary figure. There may be both 'factual' information about the portrait and speculative information and in the learning stage of Step 2 due consideration must be given to the source and status of whatever information is gleaned. Knowing that information may be speculative or only of *possible* significance to the portrait does not mean it should be ruled out, however its status should be noted. In the notes that follow speculative thoughts about who Delacroix might have had in mind when painting this young orphan girl have been deliberately included to give a feel for the sort of influences that can exist when looking *beyond the face*.

Eugene Delacroix painted this picture in 1824 at the age of twenty-six. Nothing is known about the identity of the young girl, but we know a great deal about Delacroix's early years.

From an early age, threat and loss had been a part of his life. Accidents had led to the burning of his face and arms as an infant, to a near drowning and a near poisoning as a young boy. His father died when he was only seven, though there remains to this day some dispute about the true identity of his biological father, thought more likely to be family friend Charles Maurice de Talleyrand-Perigord, politician, bishop, and diplomat, to whom he bore a striking resemblance. At the age of nine Delacroix's brother was killed in battle and he was orphaned at sixteen when his mother died. He was left in the care of his older siblings and of Talleyrand himself. Early in his artistic career Delacroix fell sick with tubercular laryngitis which plagued him throughout his life.

Having shown an interest in art from an early age, Delacroix studied art in Paris and received his first commission at the age of twenty-one, to paint the *Virgin of the Harvest* for the church of Orcement. The following year he assisted Théodore Géricault with a commission for the Cathedral church of Nantes, painting the *Virgin of the Sacred Heart*. He and Gericault had become close friends when studying art together however Géricault died suddenly in January 1824 the year in which he painted *Young Orphan Girl in the Cemetery*. Both of the church commissions had illustrated their themes with the Virgin in a strikingly soulful pose, turned away from the viewer. There are clear resonances in the pose of the young orphan girl in this portrait.

Young Orphan Girl in the Cemetery is considered by many art historians to be a preparatory work for a major painting completed the same year. Delacroix's *Massacre at Chios* (1824) depicts the Turkish massacre of the Greek population of the island of Chios. Tens of thousands were either killed, deported, or dispersed to other lands. *Massacre at Chios* is a harrowing painting showing Greeks either dead, being killed, grieving or waiting to be taken into slavery. However the young orphan girl is not visible in this painting of the massacre, so it's possible that Delacroix had a different theme in mind when painting the young orphan girl. Not only is the background a cemetery rather than a battlefield but the overall feel is consoling rather than violent and full of terror.

It's possible that Delacroix (who had recently completed the two commissions for the church), was painting a more hopeful and consoling scene, with a focus on the Christian belief in eternal life. Could it be that Delacroix had in mind the occasion recorded in the Bible when a grieving Mary Magdalene visits the cemetery where Jesus is buried? Finding his body gone from the tomb she assumes it has been stolen and so her grief intensifies. John, the gospel writer, recounts Mary turning and seeing a man who she assumes is the gardener. In the ensuing conversation Mary realises that it is Jesus who has spoken to her (having risen from the dead), a moment of profound consolation.

Though he was not a religious man, Delacroix painted at least 120 religious works, mostly during the final years of his life. He died in 1863.

3. Johnson Gideon Beharry, Emma Wesley **(Figure 15)**
Often we come to a portrait of a national or celebrity figure with 'snippets' of partial and filtered information and a range of feelings; having come across it in different places but never paid it much attention. It's important to note these as we look for further information for the learning stage of Step 2.

Born in 1979 and brought up in Grenada, Johnson's ancestors were from India, Africa and Scotland. One of eight children, Johnson had a difficult childhood; his father suffered from alcohol addiction and his mother with a disability. His grandmother was a stabilising force in his life, a 'church lady' who was 'the only person to show me love'. Encouraged by his grandmother, Johnson moved to England in 1999 and was taken in and supported by members of his family living in London.

Having got qualifications in English and Mathematics, Johnson dropped out of college education, finding he could earn good money in the building trade. He was able to live a 'fast life' — in a world of street-gangs, parties, alcohol, girls and drugs. A phone conversation with his grandmother brought him to his senses and he realised how far he'd come from his roots and how much she would disapprove of his life if she knew what it consisted of. Determined to change his ways and escape the bad influence of his friends, Johnson applied to join the army. After being told to clean up his act and improve his appearance Johnson was eventually accepted into the army and joined the Princess of Wales' Royal Regiment in 2001.

Tours of duty in Kosovo and Northern Ireland were followed by a posting to Iraq in 2004 where from the outset Johnson found himself in a warzone, under constant threat and bombardment. In May and June 2004 (on both occasions under intense enemy fire), driving a Warrior armoured vehicle, Johnson saved the lives of thirty soldiers. This was at immense personal cost – he was shot five times and received a very serious head injury from the detonation of a rocket propelled grenade in close proximity. During a five-week coma he had a near-death experience in the course of which a bright white figure told him it was time to 'go back' – and he came out of his coma.

Following brain surgery Johnson's broken eye-socket and nose were reconstructed with titanium and there followed many years of rehabilitation, forcing him to live with near constant pain, nightmares and flashbacks: he made two suicide attempts.

In 2005 he became the youngest ever recipient of the Victoria Cross – Britain's highest award for gallantry, only awarded for extreme acts of bravery in the face of the enemy.

Johnson's portrait was painted by Emma Wesley in 2006, a special commission by the National Portrait Gallery. His response to the portrait was as follows:

> *The face is really serious. Maybe at the time because I'm in uniform. When I'm in a uniform it's like a different frame of mind. Something else takes over. I guess that's why my face is like that. Maybe if I was in civilian, I would have been more relaxed, smiling, because I smile quite a lot. This is a soldier face because I remember she kept telling me 'Smile, smile, smile' but it's hard to get me to smile when I'm in uniform, I don't think a soldier should be smiling. To me, it's just a portrait. But looking at it with the Victoria Cross there's a lot more to it because the Victoria Cross represents the lives that I saved in Iraq so that means a lot to me.*

Artist Emma Wesley said in response to a question about the relationship of a painter to their subject:

> *The painter cannot be indifferent to their subject and*

should not be indifferent to world affairs. One of the difficulties of the Beharry portrait was to paint a war hero, without appearing to celebrate, or even condone, a war in which I did not believe. I thus painted Johnson as a young man who had acted very bravely but had also been very badly injured in action. As it turned out during sittings, Johnson himself was far from pro-war and his direct gaze in the portrait was intended to ask the many questions about the war which he had been denied the opportunity of putting to the government. (34)

Johnson was disappointed not to be able to return to active service as an infantry soldier, being confined instead to a desk job. So drawing from his personal experience and his passion to help others, Johnson set up the JBVC Foundation which aims to show young people there is an alternative and positive future to be found beyond gang-culture. The Foundation provides young people with a mentor who supports them with education, training, apprenticeships and work placements, helping to break cycles of reoffending, to lead them into a sustainable career and to become valued members of their community.

4. Malala Yousafzai, Shirin Neshat (Figure 16)

All of us are shaped and influenced by our familial, cultural and national heritage, some of this is conscious, much of it is unconscious. For those of us who are white and British this portrait of Malala Yousafzai may disclose aspects of how we see heritage which give us cause for reflection. However, it's important in the learning stage of Step 2 to restrain our inclination to self-analysis and evaluation and to maintain a disciplined effort simply to learn more about the subject before continuing.

Malala was born in 1997, in Mingora, Pakistan. At the time Mingora was a popular holiday destination and well known for its summer festivals. Malala attended a school founded by her father. In 2009 the Taliban took control of the area and began to close and destroy schools in a bid to prevent the education of girls over the age of eight. The Taliban believed the home to be the rightful place for girls and women, protected from harmful exposure to situations in which there might be a mixing of the sexes and a lack of both female teachers and provision for women's personal needs. Moreover, girls' further education was considered unnecessary as women were forbidden by the Taliban from seeking employment outside the home.

To protest at the threatened closure of her school, Malala began to write a blog for BBC Urdu about life under Taliban rule, writing under a pseudonym to protect herself and her family. She and her father however gradually gained a reputation for their willingness to speak out for the universal right to education, even making appearances on Pakistani talk shows and in several documentaries. In 2011 Malala was nominated for the International Children's Peace Prize and rose to national prominence after receiving the National Youth Peace Prize. She and her father both received death threats.

In October 2012 Malala was on a bus on her way home from school when a Talib gunman boarded and demanded to know which of the girls was Malala. He shot her in the head and as a result she was very badly wounded. She was treated in hospital in Pakistan before being transferred to the United Kingdom where she underwent multiple surgeries to treat her injuries.

At the time of her attack there was an international outpouring of support for Malala and over the following years her public profile increased dramatically. She took every opportunity to speak out in support of girls' education. At the age of sixteen Malala made a speech in which she began with the following:

I don't know what people would be expecting me to say. But first of all, thank you to God for whom we all are equal and thank you to every person who has prayed for my fast recovery and a new life. I cannot believe how much love people have shown me .... I do not even hate the Talib who shot me. Even if there is a gun in my hand and he stands in front of me. I would not shoot him. This is the compassion that I have learnt from Muhammad-the prophet of mercy, Jesus Christ and Lord Buddha. This is the legacy of change that I have inherited from Martin Luther King, Nelson Mandela and Muhammad Ali Jinnah. This is the philosophy of non-violence that I have learnt from Gandhi Jee, Bacha Khan and Mother Teresa. And this is the forgiveness that I have learnt from my mother and father. This is what my soul is telling me, be peaceful and love everyone. (35)

The following year Malala became the youngest person to receive the Nobel Peace Prize for her work to secure the right of all children to an education. The Prime Minister of Pakistan, Nawaz Sharif said:

She is (the) pride of Pakistan, she has made her countrymen proud. Her achievement is unparalleled and unequalled. Girls and boys of the world should take lead from her struggle and commitment. (36)

Malala used her prize money to build a secondary school for girls in Pakistan and she celebrated her eighteenth birthday by opening a school for Syrian girls in a refugee camp in Lebanon. Speaking on her first day as an adult, she demanded on behalf of the world's children, that leaders invest in books instead of bullets. Eventually she continued her own education in the United Kingdom, graduating with a degree in Politics, Philosophy and Economics from Oxford University.

Malala was named after the Afghan heroine Malalai. In 1880 when Malalai was eighteen or nineteen she joined local forces with her father and fiancée in an assault on occupying British-Indian forces near the town of Maiwand. During the battle Malalai played the traditional women's role of providing for the men and tending to the wounded, however as the fighting raged on the Afghan forces began to lose courage. Malalai took the initiative and seizing the Afghan flag she shouted: 'Young love! If you do not fall in the battle of Maiwand, By God, someone is saving you as a symbol of shame!' Later, when a lead flag-bearer was killed, Malalai went forward, held up the flag and sang a folksong:

> With a drop of my sweetheart's blood,
> Shed in defence of the Motherland,
> Will I put a beauty spot on my forehead,
> Such as would put to shame the rose in the garden!

Malalai, her father and her fiancée were all killed on the battlefield and her burial place soon became a shrine and she a national folk-hero. Scholars remain divided on how much of Malalai's story is history and how much is folklore, however schoolchildren in Afghanistan still learn about her and many schools and other institutional buildings bear her name.

Malala's portrait is one of a pair of portraits by Iranian-born artist and film-maker Shirin Neshat. Neshat took a series of photographs and hand inscribed in calligraphy a 2011 poem by the Pashto poet Rahmat Shah Sayel. The translation of the poem follows:

MALALA II: (Malala Yousafzai)
By Rahmat Shah Sayel
(*Translated by Qasim Swati*)

*O Malala I, Malala II is your reincarnation and the
new Malala of the Pakhtoons.
You can listen to your own voice when Malala II is
speaking after a long time,
as Malala II is obsessed with what you believed in and
acted upon.
As the flag made up of your red shawl is
still flying over your grave in Maiwand as
a symbol of your heroism for the sake of
your Pashtoon Nation, Malala II is also following in
your footsteps.*

As you made your Pashtoon Nation undefeatable
in the history of Maiwand by your own single tappa [a
short folk song of northern Indian origin],
Malala II is also determined, undefeated and
strong enough in carrying out her mission.
No one could break your record of bravery for the last
two generations,
but she [Malala II] did so, because she does the same
for her nation, as you did for yours.
If the people had valued you as equal to flowers
[because of your bravery and achievements], so have
the flowers themselves gifted Malala II to the people
of Pakhtunkhwa.
You might have seen the wreckage of your country,
but this Malala II is fit and proper enough to find a
solution for compensating for that wreckage.
Whatever tappa you had sung in the battlefield
of Maiwand;
that tappa had been coined and invented by Malala II,
as she is hugely inspiring.
As you encouraged the defeated and disheartened
fighters of your nation to come back to the trenches
and fight against the enemy, this is Malala II who is
determined to accomplish your mission.
While you brought a huge honour to your nation by
encouraging your countrymen to fight against the

enemy, the same battle is fought by her [Malala II]
with the help of a pen [education] to serve her nation.
You are the reflection of the poetry of Sa'eel,
but she is a light born from your reflection.

Artist Shirin Neshat recalled her meeting with Malala:

I knew of Malala as an extraordinary young woman
... when I look back on our encounter, I am left with
impressions of humility, wisdom and a rare sense of
inner beauty. (37)

EXPERIMENT

Once you have the three-step method at your fingertips you will find endless possibilities for its application in both informal and formal contexts. The following ideas for experimentation will help establish the method and reveal its benefits and limitations:

Gallery visits

When visiting a gallery, pre-select one or two portraits to look at (less is more). If it's available purchase an audio guide to help with the learning stage of Step 2. A busy gallery will prove to be a difficult place for meditation and contemplation so if possible choose a time which is likely to be the quietest.

Religious Icons

These are 'written' for the purpose of going *beyond the face* so familiarise yourself with how to appreciate and engage with an Icon and spend some time with one. If possible, find an Orthodox Church (there are many different branches, e.g. Syrian, Greek, Coptic) where you can stay for a while and spend some time in front of the Icon in the sacred context for which it was made. Failing this there are plenty of Icons available on the internet.

Portrait devices

Chapter 3 gives examples of devices used by portrait artists to go 'beyond the face'. Starting with images in the National Portrait Gallery, experiment with the three-step method on portraits where artists have used different devices to go *beyond the face*, to see how they are intended to work and how well they work for you.

Other cultures

The life-stories of artists and their subjects from other cultures can help disclose strengths and weaknesses in our own culture at points of resonance and dissonance.

Repetition

Practise with different portraits of the same subject by different artists – including more controversial artists who have got 'under the skin' of their subject and gone beyond widely accepted perceptions. Examples include Graham Sutherland's 1954 portrait of Winston Churchill, that Churchill's wife had destroyed after it was presented to him as a gift and portraits of King Henry VIII by artists other than Hans Holbein the Younger. The latter will test prevailing perceptions of a man who has been so influential in shaping the state and church in protestant England.

Lesser known

Practise with portraits by unknown artists about which there is very little information available for the learning stage of Step 2. This will help focus attention on what is seen as opposed to what you know.

Your own portraits

Practise with portraits you've made or taken yourself, including those on your phone (including self-portraits). The subjects are likely to be well known to you so discipline will be needed to notice why you have curated these. Notice what is actually in the portrait and what you relate to beyond what is obvious at first sight. Try taking self-portraits in different contexts and moods and notice variations.

Lifetime portraits

Practise with self-portraits made by an artist over a long period of time, for example those of Vincent van Gogh, Rembrandt van Rijn or Stanley Spencer. See how these shed light on their self-perception and your own self-perception in different ages and circumstances – all of our lives are in a constant state of flux.

CONCLUSION

Apart from practice and experimentation with portraits, most of us will also benefit from practising *per se* with mindfulness, meditation, and contemplation. Chapter 4 gives ideas of how, both with focussed attention and in everyday life, to make them a more natural part of our experiential, thoughtful and intuitive life. The benefits of these becoming part of our natural disposition are far-reaching – but for the purpose of this book we will become much more readily able to respond to those whom we meet both face to face and in their portraits, and so be better able to develop healthy relationships with ourselves and others.

And finally – have fun! Push the boundaries knowing there are whole new worlds to discover in experimenting with different styles of portrait in different eras and cultures and using different devices to go *beyond the face*, including the weird and wild. Smile, laugh at yourself, weep as you discover 'blind-spots' - and always be prepared to be surprised by what you didn't know that you didn't know. That's the nature of human relations, they are always full of new possibility for those with the courage to step away from what has become comfortable in its own familiarity.

CHAPTER 7
CONCLUSION

In the Western industrial era public order, economic growth and relative stability have been maintained by uneasy relationships of 'dependence' between people of different social groups: the ruling classes and the ruled classes, the more and less well-educated, the economic 'haves and the have-nots'. In the later twentieth century, we began to move on from this culture of 'dependence' through liberalisation, with the promotion of individual autonomy and respect for human rights. But we've moved little further than 'independence'; we tolerate those of other groups provided they maintain their distance. Even in the United Kingdom's multi-faith and multi-denominational church work we see a similar stagnation, a complacent satisfaction with 'independence'. By and large we tolerate people of faith with whom we differ and we work together only where it's straightforward or necessary.

In 1963, the Revd Martin Luther King Jr. had a dream:

> '*that my four little children will one day live in a nation where they will not be judged by the color of their skin but by the content of their character. I have a dream … I have a dream that one day in Alabama, with its vicious racists, with its governor having his lips dripping with the words of interposition and nullification, one day right there in Alabama little black boys and black girls will be able to join hands with little white boys and white girls as sisters and brothers.*'

Since his tragic death we have overcome the scourge of physical segregation in the USA (and indeed in many other parts of the world), but we have failed to overcome a pervasive psychological segregation. The dark social and cultural forces of discrimination and exclusion still exert their malevolent influence. The Black Lives Matter movement has exposed our failures and in the United Kingdom we are realising how the pernicious legacy of the colonial era still exerts a powerful influence. Over the same period globalisation and free market economics have deepened wealth inequalities around the world. These are being exacerbated by the all-pervasive and devastating impacts of climate change, blatantly and violently exposing the poverty of our limited progress. In our 'independence', inequalities are becoming etched ever more deeply into the social landscape and the biosphere is sounding clear alarm signals with fire and flood on an unprecedented scale. As fast as borders have been overcome through free trade and other multinational agreements so the same national borders have become tightly regulated in attempts to control human migration as people attempt to make a new life for themselves elsewhere.

It's time we moved on from personal and national 'independence' to 'inter-dependence'. It's time we recognised that creation is an evolving system and not a machine working to fixed laws, that every human being is essential to the whole. It's time we embraced inter-faith and inter-denominational church work, moving from tolerance to magnanimity, a generous mutual giving and receiving in love, for that is the best response to the image of God imprinted into each one of us.

As 'dependent' and 'independent' humans we remain strangers to each other and to the earth and the consequences are plain for all to see. If we move into 'interdependence', we will find ourselves 'coming home' to where we first belonged, to a state glimpsed in early childhood where we took each other at face value and not at the value later placed upon us by social and cultural forces.

The aim of this book has been to equip us to move into this state of 'interdependence' in our social relationships, by going beyond the faces we encounter in portraits to discover fellow human beings, those with whom we are united in body and soul in our wonderful diversity. This is to recognise that we are all made in the image of God, that we need each other if we are not to remain discontented strangers to ourselves, to others and to the earth.

Since beginning this book, artificial intelligence has introduced us to the world of deepfake and synthetic portraits in digital media. Once again the landscape is changing rapidly. If the three-step method of *noticing, responding* and *reflecting* on the person beyond a face can gain some traction for all who read this book then perhaps it will contribute to a growing sense of 'interdependence' which will become a foundation of hope for this and future generations.

To break down the dividing walls that separate people of difference by nurturing relationships of mutual generosity, is to cultivate peace; a wholeness or at-one-ness. As fellow human beings we will be no longer strangers but companions, united in love of self, of others, of God and his earth. I'll leave the last word with Jesus who said:

CONCLUSION

You shall love the Lord your God with all your heart, and with all your soul, and with all your mind, and with all your strength – and you shall love your neighbour as yourself. There is no other commandment greater than these. Mark 12v30-31

ENDNOTES

1. Jansen, L. et al. (ed.), *Vincent van Gogh – The Letters*, Amsterdam & The Hague: Van Gogh Museum and Huygens ING, 2009.
2. Jansen.
3. Davie, G. *Religion in Britain Since 1945: Believing without Belonging (Making Contemporary Britain)*, John Wiley & Sons, 1994.
4. Gormley, A. quoted in *https://artquest.org.uk/artlaw-article/gormley-on-the-beach/* Accessed 23rd March 2024.
5. Cooley, C. H. quoted in Cherry S. *Thy Will be Done*, Bloomsbury Continuum, 2020.
6. Julian of Norwich, quoted in Starr, M. *The Showings*, Hampton Roads Publishing Company, 2022.
7. Nouwen, H. *The Wounded Healer: Ministry in Contemporary Society, p.41*, Darton, Longman & Todd, 2014.

8. West, S. *Portraiture*, Oxford University Press, 2004.

9. *https://www.npg.org.uk/about/corporate/gallery-policies/collections-development-policy* Accessed 23rd March 2024.

10. Jansen.

11. Jansen.

12. Jansen.

13. Magritte, R. Cited in Torczyner H. *Magritte: Ideas and Images,* Harry N. Abrams, New York, 1979.

14. BBC TV, *Leonora Carrington The Lost Surrealist,* https://www.youtube.com/watch?v=oukpRMIPISk&t=434s, Accessed 25th April 2022.

15. Dawson, D. and Holborn, M. *Lucian Freud: A Life*, Phaidon Press, 2019.

16. Hawser, K. *Stanley Spencer*, Princeton University Press, 2001.

17. Bradley, A. Curator: *Love, Art, Loss: The Wives of Stanley Spencer*, Exhibition, Stanley Spencer Gallery, Cookham, Berkshire, 26th March to 1st November 2020.

18. BBC TV, *Newsnight,* https://www.youtube.com/watch?v=j_-3l-YlltA Accessed 26th April 2022.

19. Quinn, M. *DNA portrait of Sir John Sulston, http://marcquinn.com/artworks/single/dna-portrait-of-sir-john-sulston Accessed 26th April 2022.*

ENDNOTES

20. West.

21. Williams, M. et al. *The Mindful Way Through Depression,* Guildford Press, 2007.

22. Williams, W. and Penn, Dr D. *Mindfulness: A Practical Guide to Finding Peace in a Frantic World,* Piatkus Books, 2011.

23. Merton T. *New Seeds of Contemplation,* New Directions, 2007.

24. Merton.

25. Harter, M. G. *Hearts on Fire, Praying with the Jesuits,* Loyola University Press, 2005.

26. Hillesum, E. *An Interrupted Life: the Diaries and Letters of Etty Hillesum 1941-43,* Persephone Books Ltd, 1999.

27. Jansen.

28. Jansen.

29. Jansen.

30. Jansen.

31. Jansen.

32. Jansen.

33. Beharry, G. *Interview,* https://www.npg.org.uk/assets/files/pdf/collections/explore/by-artists-and-sitters/AGbeharry.pdf Accessed 26th March 2024.

34. Wesley, E. *Interview,* https://newlinearperspectives.wordpress.com/interviews/ew/ Accessed 26th March 2024.

35. Yousafzai, M. *Speech,* https://malala.org/newsroom/malala-un-speech Accessed 26th March 2024.

36. Sharif, N. *Speech,* https://www.vanguardngr.com/2014/10/malala-yousafzai-pride-pakistan-pm-nawaz-sharif/ Accessed 12th April 2023.

37. Neshat, S. *Interview,* https://www.npg.org.uk/collections/search/portrait/mw286089 Accessed 12/4/23.